THE CRACKS

Phil Porter

THE CRACKS IN MY SKIN

OBERON BOOKS
LONDON

First published in 2008 by Oberon Books Ltd
521 Caledonian Road, London N7 9RH
Tel: 020 7607 3637 / Fax: 020 7607 3629
email: info@oberonbooks.com
www.oberonbooks.com

A catalogue record for this book is available from the British Library.

ISBN: 978-1-84002-834-8

Printed in Great Britain by Antony Rowe Ltd, Chippenham

Characters

JANIE
female 16

JOSEFA
female 36

LINDEN
male 16

ROPER
male 70

ALUN
male 33

INGER
female 16

The Cracks in my Skin was first performed in The Studio at Manchester Royal Exchange, on 14 February 2008, with following cast:

JANIE, Mattie Houghton

JOSEFA, Claire Cox

LINDEN, Tunji Kasim

ROPER, Col Farrell

ALUN, Nick Bagnall

INGER, Anna Lauren

Director Chris Meads
Designer Hannah Clark

JOSEFA's front garden. There is no greenery, just slabs and a heart-shaped area of white pebble. Two rakes lean against the wall of the house. A front door, a window, a drainpipe and a movement-sensitive security light can also be seen. The house is at the quiet end of a quiet road.

JOSEFA is sitting on a deckchair. She wears a jacket though it is a very hot day. She has a suitcase and a packet of tissues with her.

JANIE appears on the pavement. Her face and arms are sunburnt. Her mouth is peeling away. As always, she has a packet of salt and vinegar crisps in her hand.

JANIE: Miss.

JOSEFA: Janie. (*Pause.*) What are you doing here?

JANIE: Miss, do you ever find it…like…?

> *Pause.*

JOSEFA: Sorry?

JANIE: Like…hard getting close?

JOSEFA: Are you all right?

JANIE: Getting up close.

JOSEFA: I'm sorry, I don't know what you mean.

> *They look at each other.*

I don't know what you mean, love.

JANIE: Can I hang round here for a bit? I been going for miles, my legs are like totally gone.

JOSEFA: Well /

JANIE: Can I?

JOSEFA: Just for a minute then. (*Pause.*) So. No more school, eh? Ever.

JANIE: You had your hair done different?

JOSEFA: Yeah, do you like it?

JANIE: Yeah, do you though? Find it hard? Getting close?

JOSEFA: To what?

JANIE: Got a husband?

JOSEFA: Pardon?

JANIE: Have you got a husband?

Pause.

JOSEFA: Listen, love /

JANIE: Do you though? To people? Like you can't get close as much as you need, no matter if anything. Know what I mean?

JOSEFA: Yeah, listen, it's good to see you and things…

JANIE: Because /

JOSEFA: But /

JANIE: I do. Find it difficult.

JOSEFA: Right.

JANIE: I could murder myself sometimes. (*Pause.*) I don't mean murder myself, I just mean shout at myself. Sometimes. Loudly. 'Cos the thing I desire most, than anything else, I want to get close, you know? But I can't stop blowing things apart. Vexing people like a bomb.

JOSEFA: Janie, you don't seem quite right to me.

JANIE: I'm not. Like this man Keefy says I can stay in a tent by his house for a bit.

JOSEFA: Right.

JANIE: And he's all right, Keefy and he starts coming out, you know, hot drinks and all that. But he comes out one time and we have this little kiss and I tell him that I want to wear his skin. And he's like 'eh?' So I go 'I don't mean actually wear it.' And he's like 'phew'. But I did mean wear it, and not just Keefy. 'Cos I get this thing. Like I want my head completely stuck in someone else's, perfect fit, you know? Almost Siamese. Like I got to get closer to people. But I get it all wrong, but even if I didn't, it still ain't enough, 'cos it couldn't ever be, 'cos how do you get your head in someone else's? How do you get real not loneliness with people? Smash away the glass? I want to smash the glass that's in the way, get swallowed up, wear their skin, two layers, feel warm in it, you know? Like before the birth, in the mummy, in the tiny little sac.

Pause.

JOSEFA: The thing is, Janie /

JANIE: (*Dizzy.*) Whoa, the world is like spinning.

JOSEFA: What's the matter?

JANIE: It's 'cos I fell asleep. On the hill. Jesus wept.

JOSEFA: Do you want to sit down?

JANIE: Whoa, it's like a roundabout. Why you got two rakes?

JOSEFA: Just sit down, love. Have my chair. (*JANIE sits in JOSEFA's chair. Pause.*) Better?

JANIE: (*The dizziness is subsiding.*) Whoa.

JOSEFA: Love, you don't seem very well to me.

JANIE: I don't feel the best. Why you got a suitcase?

JOSEFA: I'm going to hospital.

JANIE: When?

JOSEFA: Now. I'm waiting for a taxi. (*She clutches her face.*) Oh my God…

JANIE: What is it?

JOSEFA: Pass those tissues, will you, please? Janie?

JANIE: What's the matter?

JOSEFA: My nose is bleeding.

Blood runs down JOSEFA's fingers.

JANIE: I didn't know you got nosebleeds.

JOSEFA: I don't.

JANIE: I get nosebleeds.

JOSEFA: It's okay, I'm okay.

Pause, JOSEFA dealing with her nosebleed.

JANIE: Funny that. Me getting dizzy then you getting a
nosebleed. Miss, can I come with you? To hospital please?
I don't feel well. I feel kind of…

JANIE shows her how she feels.

Can I come to hospital with you?

Scene ends.

1:2

*JOSEFA's front garden. ROPER is cutting lengths of masking tape and
sticking them to the arm of the deckchair in which he sits. LINDEN
is picking up pebbles that have been displaced from the heart. It is
a hot day.*

ROPER: Did I tell you what happened, Linden?

LINDEN: When?

ROPER: Just this morning.

Pause.

LINDEN: No.

ROPER: Didn't I? (*Pause.*) I thought I did. (*Pause.*) I was stood
there in the precinct by the chemist, this chap comes up,
grabs me, quite threatening, he says, 'You took my blood
last year. You're that nurse.' 'Me? A nurse?' I say. 'Oh yes

you are,' he says. 'You took my blood last year and I want it back. I been getting shorter ever since.' What do you make of that? (*Pause.*) They got tuna sweetcorn, chicken and stuffing or ham and tomato. What do you reckon? Tuna sweetcorn, chicken and /

LINDEN: Who have?

ROPER: From the garage for lunch. I thought get two, have half each of each, what do you reckon? Choose one each, have half each, bit of the old choc, what do you reckon?

LINDEN takes masking tape from the arm of ROPER's chair and sticks it round the edge of a window pane, masking the glass in preparation for the painting of the frame.

It's another hot one look. I'm starting to regret wearing trousers. Look at you in your snazzy shorts, I need a pair of them myself. I'm starting to regret wearing any kind of clothes. (*Pause.*) I wish you'd say a bit more, Linden. You never used to be so quiet.

LINDEN: I'm concentrating. Doing the tape.

ROPER: Like talking to a dry stone wall it is.

LINDEN: Why've I got to talk all the time?

ROPER: Not all the time.

LINDEN: I'm doing the tape.

ROPER: Just some of it. I'm a fan of the sound of your voice. (*Pause.*) Sometimes it's like being pushed away a bit, that's all. With you not saying a word, and not wanting cups of coffee when it's me making them, then making yourself a cup soon as I'm back from the kitchen. It's like I'm being barriered off all suddenly. I get worried.

LINDEN: Well don't.

ROPER: I'm your grandad.

LINDEN: So?

ROPER: So have you just gone off me a bit then or what? 'Cos it's every day at the moment, all this quietness. I thought we were partners. I thought we were planning to have fun doing this. I thought you liked my little stories. It's like your eyes are mini pebbles all suddenly. You ain't been stealing again?

LINDEN: I already told you, I ain't ever stealing again.

ROPER: Then what? You're not reading them horror books again?

LINDEN: What horror books?

ROPER: You know what horror books before bed.

LINDEN: That was when I was like twelve.

ROPER: So what then?

LINDEN: Just…give us a bit of tape.

ROPER gives LINDEN a bit of tape and he sticks it to the window pane.

ROPER: Hey, I'll tell you something else happened this morning. I saw a little brown mouse by the toaster. Little brown mouse wearing top hat and tails, whistling 'God Save The Queen'. Conducting with a couple of cocktail sticks.

JANIE appears on the pavement.

JANIE: All right, Linden.

LINDEN: Janie.

JANIE: What you doing?

ROPER: Who's this then?

JANIE: Ain't this Miss Button's house?

LINDEN: Yeah, we're doing it up.

JANIE: What, as a surprise?

LINDEN: No, she asked us to.

ROPER: Friends from school, is it?

Pause.

JANIE: Can I hang round here for a bit? My legs are like totally gone.

ROPER: Be glad of the company, wouldn't we, Linden? (*Pause. ROPER sings.*) 'If I were a blackbird I'd whistle and sing.'

Pause. ROPER stands up.

I reckon I'll get those sandwiches, shall I?

LINDEN: It's only twelve.

ROPER: Well, what do they say about the early bird? (*Wiggles his finger to suggest 'the worm'.*) Jane, would you like a sandwich?

JANIE: Eh?

ROPER: From the garage?

JANIE: (*Unsure.*) I got crisps.

ROPER: Righty-o, just us. I'll pick both, shall I, Linden? Then you can pick both tomorrow. (*Pause.*) All right. Shan't be long.

ROPER goes off to the garage. Pause.

LINDEN: If it's about me tripping you up at the graveyard /

JANIE: You're all right /

LINDEN: 'Cos soon as your tooth cracked I felt bad.

JANIE: I ain't bothered.

LINDEN: You heard me tell them all stop laughing.

JANIE: Honest, Linden, I ain't bothered. Yonks ago, that. They done me a new one, look.

She holds her mouth open. He peers in.

Don't look at the others.

LINDEN: Sorry. (*She allows him a second look.*) Nice one.

JANIE: Anyway, it's the dead lady what you want to say sorry to. It's her grave what I bit and got blood on. You still hang round with that Inger?

LINDEN: Not really.

JANIE: Good. She despises me. She says I'm Asian. (*Pause.*) Nice here, ain't it? Secluded. So how comes you're doing it up?

LINDEN: Well you know I do graffiti, yeah?

JANIE: Yeah.

LINDEN: Got caught, didn't I? Doing like this massive big judge smoking a spliff. Got given community service. Then Miss tells them I do art, so I end up painting all warthogs and Simbas at the hospital? All round the kids' bit and the leukaemia bit? Buzz Lightyears, Flounder from *Little Mermaid*... It was all right in the end.

JANIE: Yeah?

LINDEN: Yeah, then Miss comes and visits me, 'cos she in having tests, looks at what I done, says I can do her house and all if I want.

JANIE: What, with Buzz Lightyears?

LINDEN: No, just painted white while she's in hospital. Don't really need it mind, but Grandad reckons do it anyway if that's what she wants.

JANIE: That your grandad?

LINDEN: Yeah.

JANIE: Properly? The sandwiches bloke? He ain't black.

LINDEN: So?

JANIE: If he's your grandad though.

LINDEN: It ain't like that.

Pause.

JANIE: Oh right.

Pause.

LINDEN: Yeah. It can be difficult though. Sometimes. With him. I mean my parents ain't even like dead, know what I mean?

JANIE: Kind of. (*Pause.*) I went to the hospital.

LINDEN: Yeah?

JANIE: Went with Miss yesterday. I got dehydration from sleeping in the sun too long then walking like twenty miles? Brain dried out, had me acting like a right twonk. Got to go back Friday. Get my head sliced open cos I got these miniature devil horns been growing.

LINDEN: What, really?

JANIE: Yeah, on my head, feel.

LINDEN feels JANIE's head.

Don't press down. Weird or what? Cysts. Been there yonks apparently, growing.

LINDEN: Janie.

JANIE: Yeah.

LINDEN: That thing with the community service. It weren't the graffiti. I got done for stealing headphones. But that's it now, no more stealing, no way, I've decided.

JANIE: Right. (*Pause.*) Linden.

LINDEN: Yeah.

JANIE: Reason I came, thing is, I thought Miss'd be back from hospital by now.

LINDEN: What, the day after the operation?

JANIE: Yeah, so I came over.

LINDEN: It's a big operation, she ain't going to be back next day /

JANIE: Yeah, shut up for a bit. Thing is, I was going to ask to stay. Just for a tiny while? Only she ain't here. I mean, have you got keys?

LINDEN: Eh?

JANIE: For the house?

LINDEN: Well, yeah but /

JANIE: Lend them me.

LINDEN: Eh?

JANIE: Go on.

LINDEN: I can't.

JANIE: You can.

LINDEN: He'll go mad.

JANIE: Tell him she said it's all right. Come on, Linden, don't be an anus, she likes me.

LINDEN: Yeah, but /

JANIE: I'm living in a tent, how would you like it? And you did trip me up and crack my tooth, killed like tits that did. I had to have needles, I despise needles. Go on, then we'll be even. (*Pause.*) I got horns /

ROPER appears with a bag of provisions. He is holding up a sandwich.

ROPER: Look at this. Found an egg and cress down the back of the drinks fridge.

LINDEN: Yeah?

ROPER: It's a day out of date but she gave me half price. So, let's whack this one in the freezer til she's hard as a rock, shall we, Linden?

LINDEN: Wicked.

ROPER heads down the passageway.

JANIE: (*Alarmed.*) What's he mean, whack her in the freezer?

LINDEN: Chocolate, not you.

JANIE: Oh right, yeah. Twonk, ain't I?

LINDEN takes out the keys.

LINDEN: I'll tell him she phoned to say it's okay. But just please don't mess stuff up or steal stuff or tell a single person, yeah?

JANIE: Would I? (*She takes the keys.*) She's okay, Miss, ain't she? Remember that time she had us make fruit out of clay? I done a fucking pineapple.

LINDEN: Yeah?

JANIE: Yeah. She gave me an excellent so I keep it. As one of my possessions. I just like her 'cos she's like a normal kind of person.

LINDEN: You reckon? She's got a whole big room full of dragon paintings. And dragon ornaments.

JANIE: Eh?

LINDEN: Look through the window.

Curious, JANIE peers through the window.

JANIE: Whoa, fuck me.

LINDEN: Weird or what?

JANIE: Can I go in and look round?

LINDEN: Door's to it's locked.

JANIE: Jesus wept, I want to be that room.

LINDEN: How can you be a room?

JANIE: (*Still agog, trying to see into every corner.*) Mother of shit.

LINDEN: (*Dragging JANIE away.*) Come on, let's go.

JANIE: Eh? What about your lunch?

LINDEN: I ain't hungry.

Scene ends.

1:3

A hospital ward. It is night-time and the ward is in darkness. JOSEFA can just be seen. She is sleeping in a half-sitting position. She becomes restless…

JOSEFA: No. (*Pause.*) No. (*Pause.*) Help me. Help me God. Help.

She is silent for a couple of seconds and then screams. She thrashes about in distress…

No. Help me God, help me God. Help. (*Scream.*) Help. Uh. Jesus. Help.

ALUN arrives at her bedside. He is calm and professional. He switches on a small light.

ALUN: Okay, wake up now /

JOSEFA: No.

ALUN: (*Touches her arm.*) It's all right, you're okay /

JOSEFA: (*Lashes out.*) No.

JOSEFA's body relaxes – it seems that she is waking up, though her eyes stay closed. She covers her face with her hands and lies very still.

ALUN: You're okay. Just a bad dream, it's over now. You're okay. (*Pause.*) Are you all right there? (*No answer.*) Are you all right?

ALUN touches JOSEFA's arm and she lashes out again, this time catching him in the eye with a finger. He covers his eye and stands back in some pain. She is confused, upset…

Ow. Shit.

JOSEFA: What?

ALUN: Ow.

JOSEFA: You were…

ALUN: I was trying to help.

JOSEFA: I don't know who you are.

ALUN: I'm a doctor.

ALUN takes his hand from his face. He blinks a couple of times and rubs his eye. JOSEFA watches, still in a confused state.

JOSEFA: What's wrong with your eye?

ALUN: You just hit me.

JOSEFA: Who did?

ALUN: You did.

JOSEFA: Did I?

ALUN: Yes.

Pause. ALUN rubs his eye again.

JOSEFA: What's the matter with your eye?

ALUN: You just hit me.

JOSEFA: Did I?

ALUN: (*Laughs.*) Yes. (*He sees that she is upset.*) I'm fine. Honestly. What's your name?

JOSEFA: Josefa.

ALUN: Josefa? (*She nods.*) And when was your operation, Josefa?

JOSEFA: Yesterday.

ALUN: Okay, well, in that case, you're probably still feeling a bit confused and emotional, are you? (*She nods.*) That's just the anaesthetic wearing off, okay? And maybe the pain relief you're on. But you're through the worst of it, I promise.

JOSEFA: Please don't be kind to me.

ALUN: Sorry?

JOSEFA: Please don't be kind. I can't take it, please don't be kind.

Pause.

ALUN: Okay, what I think I'll do… This isn't my ward so I'll fetch a nurse /

JOSEFA: Don't go.

ALUN: Well, what I'll do /

She grabs his arm.

JOSEFA: No, please. (*He stops.*) Please, just stay for a minute. I need to talk to you. Just for a minute, please.

Pause. He looks at her properly for the first time.

ALUN: Okay. What do you want to talk about?

JOSEFA: This planet…

ALUN: Sorry?

JOSEFA: Me, I'm a planet.

ALUN: Sorry, I don't know what you mean.

JOSEFA: But a bomb's gone off. In the capital. So the people are all dying or dead, do you know what I mean? All that's left is blood. And dust. And seagulls. People laid out in rows. It just hurts, you know? And God's there. But He doesn't look like you'd think. (*She fights back tears. Pause.*) I've got this disease.

ALUN: What disease?

JOSEFA: Endometriosis. It's everywhere. They took out one of my ovaries. With some kind of… scooper of some kind… I don't know. But there was a cricket ball.

ALUN: Sorry, I don't quite follow.

JOSEFA: On the ovary. Not a real one, I don't think… But like a cricket ball.

ALUN: Right.

JOSEFA: So they just…whipped it out.

ALUN: Okay /

JOSEFA: I only let them because they said it would help my chances. Of having a baby. Which is what I want. But it hasn't done that. It's damaged them. He said it's damaged them, do you know him?

ALUN: Who?

JOSEFA: I can't remember his name. (*Pause.*) I have a husband, you see. But he's gone…somewhere… Malawi. To construct a school. He's left me. We're getting divorced. He's gone to Malawi to construct a school. (*She closes her eyes for a moment.*) Anyway, ten years of… For ten years he tells me he's not ready. For a baby. And then he's ready. And then this. And he says he can't deal with it. Never being a dad. So we're getting divorced. (*Pause.*) And I want a baby. I really want a baby. But it'll take a miracle now. Oh God, I'm in so much pain. (*She starts to cry.*)

ALUN: Okay. It's okay, come on. (*She continues to sob.*) The thing is… working here, I see miracles all the time. And most often, they happen to good people. And you seem like a really good person to me, so /

JOSEFA: Really?

ALUN: Absolutely.

JOSEFA: What's your name?

ALUN: Alun.

JOSEFA: Please don't be kind, Alun.

She stops crying. She looks up at ALUN's face.

What happened to your eye?

ALUN: You hit me.

JOSEFA: There's blood.

ALUN tries to wipe the blood away but he cannot find it. She wipes the blood away.

ALUN: Thank you.

Scene ends.

1:4

JOSEFA'S front garden. A hot morning. The walls are whiter than before. A number of new items are present: a space hopper, an extra chair or two, a cheap and colourful garden ornament, a few empty plant pots. The effect is messy but appealing. LINDEN is spraying weedkiller down the cracks between the slabs. The front door opens and JANIE comes out of the house wearing what she slept in. For breakfast, she is having iced water and crisps. The front door remains open through all scenes until specified.

JANIE: All right, Linden. Got to go to the hospital in a bit.

LINDEN: Yeah?

JANIE: Get the old horns removed. Shitting it something chronic I am. It's well unpleasant apparently. They slice it right down deep as the skull apparently.

LINDEN: Nasty.

JANIE: Shitting it I am. (*Pause.*) Reckon I should ask them whack a bit of snow in too while they're in there. Hot as tits, ain't it? Woke up in a puddle of sweat. (*Pause.*) Crying in there he is.

LINDEN: Who is?

JANIE: Who do you think? He's wiped the same bowl like sixty-three million times. He reckons you called him an annoying old flump.

LINDEN: So what if I did?

JANIE: And he reckons you keep calling him Roper not Grandad.

LINDEN: Roper's his name, ain't it?

JANIE: Yeah, but Linden.

LINDEN: What?

JANIE: Don't be an anus, call him Grandad, that's what he is.

LINDEN: I ain't the fucking anus, it's him, he's the fucking anus. He should learn not to muddle round in things that ain't even his fucking right.

JANIE: Eh?

LINDEN: Shouldn't he?

JANIE: What's happened?

LINDEN: Nothing. Just I seen the reality of it. And it's all brewed up.

JANIE: What has?

LINDEN: Him taking the easy route.

Pause.

JANIE: Is this about the hanging baskets?

LINDEN: Don't be a twonk all your life.

JANIE: Then what then?

LINDEN: It's about my mum and dad. It's about him seeing one tiny ice cream tub and acting like a nuclear bomb hit just cos he ain't got no one to go on at after Grandma.

Pause.

JANIE: Linden, I ain't being funny, but if you want me to be a help, yeah? You got to explain things just a tiny bit clearer.

LINDEN: Right… My mum and dad, they lived in a house, all right? With me, their son. And the house is a tiny bit on the messy side, yeah? Because, as it happens, they're messy kinds of people.

JANIE: I'm messy.

LINDEN: So, the toilet goes and breaks, and it's winter, and it's night-time, so dad has a piss in a ice-cream tub, yeah? And it's sitting there next morning when some dick social worker man turns up, hardly even announced, sniffs it, says 'Oh, we'll swipe Linden off you if you carry on like this.' And they go 'Shit', so Grandad goes, 'Oh, oh, I'll take Linden off your hands if that's any kind of help.' So they all go, 'Fine then, phew, okay, sorted.'

JANIE: So why you cheesed off with Roper?

LINDEN: 'Cos he made it too easy's what I've come to realise. For them to just go, 'Fine then, phew, have him.' And now they've gone to this town Honeybourne. I don't even see them. They ain't even together. They don't even speak to each other. They've gone to some unknown place called Honeybourne for entirely separate reasons. I mean, how peculiar is that?

JANIE: Is peculiar.

Pause.

LINDEN: Made it too easy's what I'm coming to realise.

JANIE: Linden though.

LINDEN: What?

JANIE: Well, he's all right, your grandad. I mean, holy God, he adores you like tits, don't he? And that ain't a thing to be estimated. 'Cos he'd only have took you 'cos he loved you, think about that.

LINDEN: But he made it too easy /

JANIE: And if your house was like…full of tubs of piss.

LINDEN: One tub, half full /

JANIE: 'Cos don't get me wrong, my mum's house is like some natural disaster zone. But he could have gone in the sink, not left it balanced on the sideboard. I mean, I'm only commenting, but he might probably have been worried about you, your grandad. 'Cos I know you don't speak masses but you two are close. And it's closeness what matters. Jesus fucking God, if I had someone like that, you know? Some actual man person that I could hold their head in my hands in front of me. And sort of…

She presses an imaginary skull into her own.

'Cos that's all anything's about I reckon. Grabbing at people and climbing inside them a bit. And that's what you got with your grandad. 'Cos you could chop off his fingers and suck out the blood and he still wouldn't be angry, know what I mean? (*Pause.*) When did it happen? With the ice cream tub?

LINDEN: Six years?

JANIE: Six years? Holy tits, you hold a grudge, why's it streaming out now?

LINDEN: I don't know, do I? Just being at the hospital. Like what if I get leukaemia? Is it just a little white old man bringing me grapes and that's it? And with them parading off to Honeybourne all suddenly. And anyway, everything ain't for some colossal reason, some things just brew up.

JANIE: Well, he loves you like complete mad's all I'll say on the subject. You should see him in there. Drying up the bowls like some bruised puppy. (*Pause.*) Oww.

LINDEN: Eh?

25

JANIE: Oww fucking oww.

LINDEN: Eh, what you doing?

JANIE: Bastard stung me.

LINDEN: What did?

JANIE: Wasp. Little shit-head. Fucking shit-head.

LINDEN: You all right?

JANIE: There it is. Fucking anus.

LINDEN: That ain't a wasp, it's a bee.

JANIE: How dare it?

LINDEN: You ain't allergic?

JANIE: I don't know, do I? I never been stung before. Ow though. (*She grips her leg.*) Right on the leg. Bastard. I could kill it.

LINDEN: It's going to die now anyway.

JANIE: Good. Anus.

LINDEN: Has it left the sting in?

JANIE: What do you mean?

LINDEN: The sting, it leaves it in normally.

JANIE: (*Sees the sting.*) Oh my God, it's left it in.

LINDEN: Come here, I'll pull it out.

JANIE: What's that on the end?

LINDEN: That's the poison sac.

JANIE: Oh my God.

LINDEN: Come here, I'll pull it out.

JANIE: No. It's going to hurt.

LINDEN: Not as much as leaving it in. Come on, I'll be gentle.

JANIE: Linden.

LINDEN: It won't hurt. I promise.

JANIE reluctantly lets LINDEN approach the sting.

JANIE: I despise this kind of thing. I despise it.

LINDEN: Don't worry, I'll look after you.

JANIE: If you touch it, don't it sting you and all?

LINDEN: Not if you're careful.

He gently removes the sting.

There.

JANIE: Thanks.

LINDEN: Told you I'd be gentle. How you feeling?

JANIE: Shit, my blood's bumping through it like tits.

LINDEN: Ice is good for it.

JANIE: Ice?

LINDEN: Yeah. If you hold it against it.

He takes ice from her glass.

JANIE: You do it. I'm strange when it comes to extremes of temperature.

He holds the ice against the sting. As the ice melts he begins to slide it across her inner thigh in circles. A serious, erotic moment.

My legs are well fat.

The ice melts away. ROPER comes out of the house and gets on with things.

LINDEN: Grandad.

ROPER: Yes, Linden?

LINDEN: Sorry I been acting peculiar. I didn't mean to make you feel barriered off. I mean, I meant it, I just wish I never done it. Sorry.

ROPER: That's all right, Linden.

Scene ends.

1:5

At the hospital. ALUN stands over JANIE. He wears goggles and a mask and holds a scalpel. JOSEFA sits on a chair some distance away wearing a dressing gown and slippers, holding JANIE's hand.

ALUN: Okay, is that better now Miss Button's here?

JANIE: This is going to kill, I know it is.

JOSEFA: You'll be okay.

ALUN: It won't hurt, I promise. I've used lots of anaesthetic.

JANIE: Can't she sit closer?

ALUN: No, I think Miss Button had better stay there.

ALUN slices open JANIE's horny scalp with a scalpel. He then puts the scalpel down and sets about manually expressing the greasy, foul-smelling liquid from JANIE's scalp. JANIE lets out a yelp of pain…

JANIE: Ow. Flipping hell, fuck.

JOSEFA: You're okay.

JANIE: You said it wouldn't hurt.

ALUN: Nice and still.

JANIE: What's that smell? It fucking stinks.

ALUN: That's what we're getting rid of.

JANIE: That ain't coming out of me, it reeks, Jesus, ow.

JOSEFA: (*As the smell hits her.*) Oh my God.

JANIE: (*Writhes.*) Ow.

ALUN: Okay, try and stay a bit more still.

JANIE: It's like he's tugging my fucking brain out.

JOSEFA: You're doing really well.

JANIE: He said it wouldn't hurt. He promised, the fucking anus.

JOSEFA: How long does it take?

ALUN: Just a few minutes.

JANIE: A few minutes? (*She starts to cry.*)

JOSEFA: Come on, let's talk about something else.

JANIE: I love you, Miss.

JOSEFA: Thank you, Janie.

JANIE: You're the best teacher in the world. I want to be you.

JOSEFA: That's a sweet thing to say.

JANIE: I still got my pineapple. (*Yells.*) Ow.

ALUN: (*Stops.*) Sorry.

JANIE: Fuck.

ALUN: Sorry.

JANIE: That really fucking hurt.

JANIE reluctantly allows ALUN to continue. He works in silence for a few seconds…

I despise this kind of thing, I really fucking do.

JOSEFA smiles sympathetically. Pause.

JOSEFA: Is your mum picking you up?

JANIE: I ain't living at my mum's.

JOSEFA: You're not still living in that tent?

JANIE: No.

JOSEFA: So where are you living?

JANIE: Ow.

ALUN continues in silence for a few seconds.

ALUN: So when are they sending you home, Miss Button?

JOSEFA: I don't know yet.

JANIE: Ow.

Pause.

ALUN: I'll come and find you later on if you like. If you want to talk some more.

JOSEFA: Okay.

JANIE: (*Yells.*) Ow.

She pulls away from ALUN. She stares at him for a moment, then walks off in disgust.

JOSEFA: I'll get her. She won't go far.

JOSEFA follows JANIE out. Scene ends.

1 : 6

JOSEFA'S front garden. In addition to the other things, there is a sun umbrella bearing the name of a brand of lager, some rainbow-coloured windmills, a blanket and a colourful, unfilled paddling pool. There is a hose leading out of the passageway into the pool. The chairs are arranged around the pool. A portable CD player and a blue plastic bag with a bottle in it are on the ground near the pool.

JANIE is inflating the paddling pool, blowing hard through the valve. The job is nearly done. She is tired and red-faced. She stops to use an asthma inhaler. She blows twice more then closes the valve. ROPER appears from the passageway.

ROPER: Now where did I stick that wheelbarrow of mine? Oh yes, there it is.

He grabs her ankles and walks her about the place wheelbarrow-style.

JANIE: Roper.

ROPER: Now let's go and fill it with manure, shall we?

JANIE: Roper, you anus.

ROPER: Then fill it to the brim with wriggling maggots /

JANIE: Sod /

ROPER: And dirty worms, wasn't it?

JANIE: Anus, I'll murder you, the slabs are baking.

ROPER sings 'In Dublin's Fair City' and swings JANIE from side to side. Janie joins in with the song. LINDEN comes out of the house and watches them…

ROPER: Don't mind us, Linden. Just acting like twonks.

LINDEN: (*Points to paddling pool.*) What's that for?

JANIE: That's a paddling pool, Linden. It's for whacking your feet in. All we need now's a tiny bit of water.

She goes into the house.

ROPER: Oh, she's off, the mad one's off.

Pause. LINDEN and ROPER are less comfortable without JANIE.

LINDEN: Should have seen her at school. She went round with one of them things for flipping eggs with, whacking people's legs. Even teachers, way mental she was.

ROPER: It's filling up, look.

JANIE: (*Off.*) Is it coming out?

ROPER: It's coming out.

She comes back and takes a bottle of gin from the plastic bag.

JANIE: So, what I reckon, we fill it with water, gulp down some of this stuff, then we sit in the sun with our feet in the pool till our heads fall off.

ROPER(*Inspects the gin.*) I hope you didn't steal this.

JANIE: Get lost, Roper, would I?

She goes into the house. Pause.

ROPER: 'Hayden's Excellent Gin'. Strong stuff, looks like. (*Sniffs at it.*) Lord Almighty.

JANIE returns having turned the water off.

JANIE: Give it here.

JANIE drinks gin from the bottle.

ROPER: Steady on.

JANIE: Don't worry, I been drinking it from birth. Linden?

LINDEN: Can I have something else, please?

JANIE: Don't be a child, Linden, drink. Don't mind him getting a bit drunken, do you, Roper? Being as it's in the name of celebration.

ROPER: Oh, it's a celebration, is it? What's it a celebration for?

JANIE: For me losing my horns, and you two being friends again, and Miss being nearly better.

ROPER: You can have a bit, long as you don't go mad. (*LINDEN drinks.*)

JANIE: Roper. (*ROPER drinks.*)

ROPER: Lord Almighty.

JANIE: Me again.

ROPER: I got some apple juice in the… (*JANIE drinks.*)

JANIE: Linden again. (*LINDEN drinks.*) Roper. (*ROPER drinks.*) Me again /

ROPER: Let's just hold fire for a tick, shall we?

JANIE: Why?

ROPER: Well, it ain't going nowhere. Let's get our feet in that water, cool ourselves off a bit.

JANIE and ROPER take their shoes and socks off.

LINDEN: I got a verruca but I could like keep my shoes on.

JANIE: Don't be a twonk, Linden. We don't care. I had horns
and he's your grandad. And anyway, I adore verrucas, take
them off.

*LINDEN takes his shoes and socks off. They put their feet in the
water.*

ROPER: Oh that is good. That is pleasant and cooling. Very
good.

JANIE: Told you. Sit on your chairs, boys.

*The boys sit on their chairs. JANIE presses play on the tape player.
The song – James Taylor's 'Shower The People' – is midway through.
JANIE sits. ROPER closes his eyes.*

Perfect. (*Pause.*) Do you think anyone can see us?

ROPER: I doubt it.

JANIE: I want them to. I want them to think we're complete,
utter insaniac mental-heads. Why don't you take your top
off, Linden?

LINDEN: Eh?

JANIE: Go on, take it off. I ain't never seen a black boy's body
up close.

*She takes her top off to reveal a green bra. LINDEN takes his top off.
JANIE has a look.*

I still don't get you two being different colours.

ROPER: Well, Linden's Nan and Grandpa on his father's side
are black. And my Blossom was a black girl /

JANIE: Don't lie.

ROPER: I'm not.

JANIE: Fuck me. So did you get spat at for mixing up the
races?

ROPER: On occasion.

JANIE: I love you Roper. Dirty sod. (*Pause.*) Beam on me, Mister Sun. Fill me to the brim. Burn my skin with your ultra-violent rays.

'Shower The People' ends. 'My Uncle Used To Love Me But She Died' by The Wind In The Willows begins.

Oh God, this is the world's best song.

She turns the music up and stands in the water. She dances to the cello introduction as if having a transcendental experience...

I adore it. My dad used to play it me before he left.

The music becomes fast and wild. JANIE dances and sings the first two verses of the song.

Dance with me, Linden.

LINDEN: Get lost.

ROPER: What's this?

JANIE: Don't be a child. (*She pulls LINDEN to his feet.*) Dance like me.

LINDEN copies JANIE. ROPER claps rhythmically. JANIE sings along to the third verse of the song.

Get up Roper, you dance too.

ROPER: Me?

JANIE: Yeah, come on.

ROPER: Oh, no... I'll slip over.

JANIE: You won't.

ROPER: I'll do my hip.

JANIE: Get up. Don't be a cabbage.

She pulls ROPER to his feet and he dances. They are all enjoying themselves now, splashing about and attempting to sing along. The solemn cello returns.

JANIE coaxes the others into a swaying group hug. JOSEFA arrives, unseen by the others, looking frail. She watches as they sway boozily and sing along to the final words of the song.

The music stops.

JOSEFA: Hello there.

ROPER, JANIE and LINDEN are startled.

ROPER: Oh, God. Miss Button.

JOSEFA: What are you doing?

ROPER: Oh dear, I am sorry. It being such a hot one, we thought we'd have a little party but that was too raucous.

JOSEFA: Where did you find that paddling pool?

ROPER: It was under Janie's bed.

JOSEFA: It was under my bed.

JANIE: Yeah, 'cos I been sleeping in your bed.

JOSEFA: You've been staying in my house?

JANIE: Kind of.

ROPER: You did say she could.

JANIE: Yeah, weeny bit of a fib, that, actually, Roper.

ROPER: Oh God.

JANIE: I thought she was coming out Friday. I ain't broke nothing.

ROPER: That's not the point.

JANIE: I been respectful.

ROPER: That's very naughty.

JANIE: I didn't even get in the bed, I just slept in my clothes.

JOSEFA: But those are my clothes. That's my bra.

ROPER: Oh God, I am sorry. Linden, did you know about this?

LINDEN: (*Unconvincing.*) No.

ROPER: Linden, I'm disappointed in you.

JOSEFA: It doesn't matter, it's done now.

LINDEN: I didn't know she was coming back today.

ROPER: That's hardly the point /

JOSEFA: (*Sharp.*) I said leave it, the damage has been done. (*Pause.*) I need to sit down.

ROPER: Linden…

LINDEN puts a chair behind JOSEFA. They are all desperate to please her. Silence.

JOSEFA: Could I have some of your drink, please?

ROPER: Linden, fetch a fresh beaker from the kitchen. (*LINDEN heads for the door.*) Down the passage, Linden, save the carpet getting grubby. (*LINDEN goes down the passageway.*) Got a favourite beaker, Miss Button?

JOSEFA: Not really.

ROPER: (*Calls.*) Any beaker. (*Pause.*) I've got apple juice if you want to damp it down a bit.

JOSEFA: No, thank you.

ROPER: I'm sorry it's so messy out here. I know you wanted it tidy.

JOSEFA: It doesn't matter.

JOSEFA looks around her. The transformed garden amuses her – she would laugh but it would hurt. LINDEN comes back with a cup. ROPER pours some gin and they all watch JOSEFA drink.

You can sit down.

They sit. LINDEN puts his t-shirt back on. Pause.

ROPER: Well, we got the painting done. Oh, and we did you some hanging baskets.

JANIE is staring sulkily at the contents of a little clear plastic bag.

ROPER: What you get there, love?

JANIE: Nothing.

ROPER: What is it?

JANIE: It's the pus bags from my head, the horns, the doctor gave them me.

Pause.

ROPER: Just got to clear the back garden now. There's three tin baths back there. All woodlice and slow-worms underneath. Cooling the blood.

Pause. JOSEFA drinks. Pause.

Slick, slim slippers sliding south. (*Pause.*) When I was young I was a keen player of billiards. Did I ever tell you this, Linden?

LINDEN: Eh?

ROPER: That's right, and I was playing with my old friend Bish one day, and he hit one, it shot up off the baize and bonked me clonk on the chest, whack, right there. And I got a bruise where it hit. Big bruise all purple and shiny like a… Not a courgette, the other one.

JOSEFA: An aubergine?

ROPER: Thank you, Miss Button. Our American cousins call it the egg plant. (*Pause.*) Well, from that bruise, what should grow but a person's ear, quite small at first /

JANIE: Eh?

ROPER: A person's ear.

LINDEN: (*To JOSEFA.*) It's a story. He made it up, he tells them all the time.

ROPER: I tell it 'cos it's true, I swear, it grew clean out the bruise. I said nothing at first, being embarrassed, but events took a further peculiar turn. I could hear this voice through it. Hushed little voice at first it was, but it gradually picked up strength, and the things it said. 'There shalt be flooding up in the north' I heard it say, and sure enough, much of Scotland was under water inside a week /

JANIE: Roper, you're such a twonk.

ROPER: It's true.

JANIE: Ignore him, Miss. He's a loony bin /

ROPER: 'Rest not in thy gardens,' it said, and that day a rock fell out of the sky and bonked a lady's foot as she rested in her garden, much as Miss Button is resting in her garden now.

JANIE: Yeah yeah /

ROPER: Well, with great power comes great responsibility and I was in demand. Prime Minister's on the phone. 'Should we do this war, Roper? Should we do that war, Roper?' People wanting weather reports for the cricket. And every time the ear came good. Well, it's no exaggeration to say that for a time I was the world's most important person, and by some distance.

JANIE: In your dreams.

ROPER: Well /

JANIE: Don't tell us. It was God's voice.

LINDEN: It didn't really happen, it's a story.

JANIE: That's what I mean, in the story.

ROPER: Well /

LINDEN: It didn't happen.

ROPER: Well. After a time the ear got old and droopy and the voice got hard to hear. I kept hearing these babbling voices, like Indians mixed in. I did as best I could, had a giant deaf aid fitted, all that, but one or two mistakes crept in. I misheard something about Mr Hitler posing no significant threat. Something else about the moon landings. Before I knew it, the world had me out on my bum. My powers were gone. The ear fell off, I met Blossom, God rest her soul, started working for Customs and Excise. Fact is, I'd forgot all about it until just the other day when… Well, see if you think this is strange.

He turns away from them all and unbuttons his shirt.

JANIE: What's he doing?

ROPER: It's embarrassing really, but as I'm among trustworthy friends, and if you promise not to laugh.

JOSEFA: We won't laugh.

ROPER: Okay. Three. two. one.

ROPER turns and roars, opening his shirt to reveal a massive drawn-on ear on his chest. JANIE and JOSEFA laugh. LINDEN is both amused and horrified.

LINDEN: Oh my God /

JANIE: Roper you twonk /

LINDEN: Grandad, that is so embarrassing /

LINDEN goes into the house.

ROPER: What do you reckon?

JANIE: We reckon you're a mad old twonk.

ROPER: What do you reckon, Miss Button?

JOSEFA: Very good /

ROPER: I drew it on earlier to make people laugh.

JANIE: You are one deranged anus.

ROPER: I'll tell you another in a bit.

JANIE: Mad as tits is what you are.

ROPER: So there we have it.

JANIE: And you got tits, look at them.

ROPER: Any more to drink, Miss Button?

JOSEFA: Thank you.

Scene ends.

1 : 7

JOSEFA's dragon room. Deep shelves run round the room from floor to ceiling, displaying hundreds of dragon ornaments and items of dragon paraphernalia. There are puppets, sculptures, carvings, paintings and items of jewellery. The items have been arranged with great care by someone with an artistic eye. The effect is magical.

With a key in one hand and some crisps in the other, JANIE enters the room. She is totally enchanted – by the room, by the day she is having, by life. She spins on the spot, trying to take in the beauty of the place in all its panoramic glory. ROPER appears with an envelope in his hand. It is the first time he has been in the dragon room too.

ROPER: Flip me.

JANIE: Beautiful, ain't it?

ROPER: Lord above.

JANIE: She said I could come in whenever I like.

ROPER: So many different things.

JANIE: Why do you think she loves dragons so much?

ROPER: Why does anyone love anything?

JANIE: I reckon she loves them for the flared-up nose-holes.

They look around, peer at things. ROPER turns his attention to JANIE.

ROPER: I got something for you.

ROPER holds out the envelope. JANIE takes it and opens it...

JANIE: Don't tell me, it's a Christmas card in the middle of summer. You reckon you're humorous but actually you're gay.

ROPER: No, not a Christmas card, it's a thanks card.

JANIE: Thanks for what?

ROPER: Read it.

JANIE: Twonk, thanks for what? (*She reads.*) 'Janie, you've been very much a force for the good since showing up a few days back though it seems a great deal longer.' Why do old men write slopey like they're dying?

ROPER: 'Cos we are dying.

JANIE: 'Thanks for persuading Linden that his interests were all I ever acted in and he told me it was you so there's no point denying it, so thanks again from Roper.' Cheers, Roper. I hardly ever get cards.

ROPER: (*Deals her three vouchers.*) And five, ten, fifteen pounds of vouchers.

JANIE: Fuck me, I never get presents.

ROPER: It's Debenhams.

JANIE: You generous anus.

ROPER: Get what you like with them. I'm no real expert on what young ladies want these days, so I thought it best you go and choose yourself.

JANIE: Cheers for that, Roper. Long as you don't start pulling my pants down suddenly.

ROPER: Eh? What did you say that for?

JANIE: Old man giving gifts.

ROPER: That's not what this is.

JANIE: I know.

ROPER: So what did you go and say that for?

JANIE: I don't know, it's just a comment. Some men give out gifts then reckon they can yank down your knickers.

ROPER: If I give you a present it's 'cos I want to, not 'cos I want something back. I don't want anything to do with your knickers.

JANIE: Yeah, I know you fucking don't. I don't even know why I said it, so shut up, 'cos I never even meant to speak. I ain't even wearing any knickers.

ROPER: (*Horrified.*) Janie.

JANIE: What?

Pause.

ROPER: Well, I'm very grateful is what that's about. So if you need anything, you come to me. 'Cos, you know, vouchers don't cover it.

They go back to looking at the dragons. JANIE stops.

JANIE: Can I bite your arm?

ROPER: Eh?

JANIE: Can I bite your arm?

ROPER: You want to bite my arm?

JANIE: You did say anything.

ROPER: Well…Yeah but /

JANIE: Not so it bleeds, just lightly.

ROPER: You really want to bite my arm?

JANIE: Not bite it, just hold it in my mouth like a dog.

ROPER: What for?

JANIE: You can tell me to stop if it hurts. (*Pause.*) Go on.

ROPER: I suppose there's no real harm in it /

JANIE: Legend. Take your shirt off.

ROPER: Oh, no, I don't think /

JANIE: Come on, there's no point unless it's the top bit. (*She helps ROPER slip his arm out of his shirt.*) The top bit's soft as tits, it's like turkey.

ROPER offers his bicep. JANIE gently bites into it.

ROPER: In all my life, never did I imagine I'd fetch up in a room full of dragons having my arm bit by a young girl. (*She bites harder.*) Oww, that… Stop, that hurts, that bloody hurts. (*He shakes her off.*) Flip me, Janie /

JANIE: Sorry, I got a bit carried away.

ROPER: I'll say you did.

JANIE: Get me back if you want.

ROPER: No thanks.

JANIE: Bite my arm.

ROPER: No thanks.

JANIE: Bite it, else I ain't going to live with myself. (*He bites her arm for a second.*) Don't be a twonk, bite for longer. (*He bites her arm for longer.*) Perfection. You're the tits, you are, Roper.

ROPER: I'm glad you think so. Now let's just look at the ornaments, can we? Silly little nutjob.

Scene ends.

1 : 8

JOSEFA's front garden. It is night-time. JOSEFA is sitting with her feet in the paddling pool. She is lit by the movement-sensitive security lamp. LINDEN comes out of the house.

LINDEN: Miss? My grandad's doing his headstand trick in the hall if you fancy it. Ain't much of a trick, it's just a headstand, I wouldn't bother if I were you, but yeah, he wanted me to say.

JOSEFA: Thanks, Linden.

The security light goes off.

LINDEN: You all right? (*Pause.*) Want me to go away?

JOSEFA: You're okay.

LINDEN: Want me to like sit with you?

JOSEFA: If you like.

LINDEN sits. Light on. Pause.

LINDEN: So what operation was it? That you had?

JOSEFA: It's like a…removal.

LINDEN: What of?

JOSEFA: You know. Like a…growth.

LINDEN: What do you mean?

JOSEFA: You know, something that's grown that shouldn't have.

LINDEN: Oh right. (*Pause.*) I never had an operation, what's it like?

JOSEFA: I don't remember, I was asleep, thank God.

LINDEN: Yeah, but what's the…like the order of it?

JOSEFA: Well, you lie in bed and the nurse comes over and he asks you questions /

LINDEN: What, the nurse is a man?

JOSEFA: This one was. He was Spanish. So, he asks you for your date of birth and stuff like that. Does your blood pressure and that kind of thing /

Light off. JOSEFA turns. Light on.

Then the surgeon comes and speaks to you about what he's planning. Draws lines on you with his pen. Then the nurse comes back and tells you to go to the loo /

LINDEN: What if you don't need it?

JOSEFA: Well, I think they still ask you to try. So you don't pee all over them midway through, I suppose.

LINDEN: (*Laughs.*) Yeah.

JOSEFA: Then it's down in the lift to the operating place, more questions, same ones as upstairs, date of birth… Then the anaesthetist sticks the needle in. And then I got this metal taste. This frozen feeling rushing up through my body. Then all I can remember, he said, 'Let me know when you're unconscious,' and that was it.

Light off. JOSEFA waves at the sensor. Light on.

Next I knew, I felt like I'd been gone at with a bread knife. Like they'd taken my insides out, rubbed them all over with sandpaper and randomly stuffed them back in.

LINDEN: I cut the top of my thumb off once. In a door, by the hinges? Bleeded like mental it did. Sat in some taxi with this chopped-off chunk in some…purple deodorant lid. About a third of an inch.

JOSEFA: How big's a cricket ball?

LINDEN: Cricket ball? Don't know precisely. About like a fist, I reckon. Or like a medium-size orange with sewing round it. Why?

JOSEFA: No reason.

LINDEN: I like your bracelet.

JOSEFA: It's was my mum's. She's dead now. I wear it when I wish she was close by.

LINDEN: What's that on it?

JOSEFA: It's a wyvern. It's like a dragon that's quite like a bird. But with a snakey tail.

LINDEN: How old were you when she died?

JOSEFA: Same age as you are. She died on my sixteenth birthday.

LINDEN: What, really? Man, sixteenth birthday, that's harsh that is.

JOSEFA smiles. Light off.

JOSEFA: Linden. Do you ever kind of…? I don't know. I mean… Do you know what you want?

LINDEN: Eh?

JOSEFA: From…everything.

Pause.

LINDEN: Eh?

LINDEN raises an arm. Light on.

JOSEFA: Is there any single thing? That you want? From the future? Like a single thing that you need or want?

LINDEN: Not that I can think of.

JOSEFA: Like a /

LINDEN: Not massively /

JOSEFA: Ambition or a picture of… Or a passion or a picture of how you want life to turn out? I mean, do you…have anything like that?

LINDEN: Not really. (*Pause.*) I like Formula One. The car races? But I ain't even driven a normal car yet.

Light off. LINDEN moves. Light on.

Light keeps going on and off.

JOSEFA: Do you want to know what I want?

LINDEN: Go on then.

JOSEFA: To be a mum?

LINDEN: Yeah?

JOSEFA: But I've got this problem. This condition. I've got this tissue, growing, everywhere. It's the same stuff that bleeds when girls have periods, womb tissue, only I've got it all over the place. That's what this growth was. I've even got it in my nose.

LINDEN: Yeah?

JOSEFA: I mean, it's not like I'm dying, you know? It's just… my chances of a baby are getting quite remote. And now my husband's gone to Africa to mend schools. And when you've had, your whole life, people saying, 'Oh, you'll be a good mum, be a lovely mum, it'll be a fortunate baby gets you as its mum…' It affects your thoughts, you know? It affects them a lot. When, all of a sudden, all you can see ahead of you is…decades of teaching other people's kids to draw…empty bottles and kiwi fruits. All I want is a table.

LINDEN: We've got a table you can have.

JOSEFA: No, my dream. It's a table. In a garden. With food on it. And there's a man at the table, and a child at every other place. Six, eight, ten, however many children. And I'm bringing food and clearing plates. God, I'm so Victorian.

LINDEN: Have you explored alleyways like adoption?

JOSEFA: It's not what I want.

Light off. LINDEN waves. He stands and waves some more.

LINDEN: Ain't working. Is it run off a battery?

JOSEFA: No, it's plugged in.

JOSEFA stands. They wave together. They are like a pair of shipwrecked survivors on a desert island, waving wearily and without real hope at a far-off boat. Light stays off.

LINDEN: Was working before. Just stopped working, didn't it? Must have cottoned onto what we was doing.

LINDEN puts his hand against the sensor. JOSEFA sits with her feet in the water. Pause.

Actually… Actually…

JOSEFA: Yeah?

LINDEN: Can I say something sort of deranged?

JOSEFA: If you like.

LINDEN: Because actually… Sometimes I've imagined what it might be like… If you were…

JOSEFA: If…?

LINDEN: My mum.

JOSEFA: Really?

LINDEN: Yeah. I used to imagine it quite a lot. Going on… Us going on like…holidays and stuff? Things a bit like that? Or fruit picking? Be quite decent I used to think.

JOSEFA: Really?

LINDEN: Yeah. (*Pause.*) Kind of. (*Pause.*) Yeah.

JOSEFA: Why me?

LINDEN: 'Cos you're like a normal person. Except the dragons. (*She laughs.*) And 'cos you can be strict. Like when I was wasting the clay? I mean, God, it ain't nothing pervy. I used to hate it when kids said they wanted to like have sex with you in different positions or whatever. 'Cos of this thing of sometimes imagining you were my mum. (*Pause.*) I can't believe I'm saying all this out loud.

JOSEFA: I don't mind. I like it.

LINDEN: It's just my mum, she ain't exactly like a mum? She don't even let me touch her. She don't say, 'How's your day?' or any of that.

JOSEFA: Right.

LINDEN: She don't even phone since she moved. I used to see her once a week, but now it's like never. And I'm only sixteen. She don't even want to know if I like… successfully completed my community service, doing retakes, got a girlfriend, any of that. Total joke it is. Right old fucking complete and total joke my life is at the moment, total joke I am.

JOSEFA: You're not.

LINDEN: No birthday card, no nothing, what am I meant to make of that? And imagine?

JOSEFA: Come here.

LINDEN: Just ignores me like I'm something to ignore, well, I ain't, 'cos I ain't fully grown. One big old fucking joke it is.

JOSEFA: Sit here.

LINDEN sits with JOSEFA, his feet in the water. She strokes his head.

It's all right.

He cries into her breast. Light on.

It's okay, it's all right. Poor baby, it's okay. You're not a joke, you're beautiful. You're so beautiful. I'm here and I'll take care of you, come on.

JANIE comes out of the house.

JANIE: What's the matter?

JOSEFA: Everything's fine.

JANIE: Linden, you all right?

LINDEN: I'm all right.

JOSEFA: Come and sit with us if you like.

JANIE sits in the water and clings to JOSEFA's legs.

You'll get cold.

JANIE: I won't. (*Silence.*) Roper, come outside.

ROPER(*Off.*) What's this?

JANIE: Come outside.

ROPER comes out of the house.

ROPER: Oh.

JANIE: Come and sit with us. (*He sits with them and holds JANIE's hand.*) This is it now. This is all there is now. From now on, we look after each other. With nothing in between, like one single person. This is it now forever.

Light off. Scene ends. Interval.

2:1

JOSEFA's front garden. A sunny September day. ROPER is dozing on a deckchair. He wears a snazzy pair of shorts. Four beakers, some used wrapping paper, two books, a new set of screwdrivers and a pair of slippers lie on the ground beside him.

JANIE, JOSEFA and LINDEN come out of the house. JANIE holds a plate of Marmite-covered crumpets. Each crumpet has a burning candle sticking out of it. JOSEFA holds four smaller plates. They sing 'Happy Birthday', waking ROPER…

ROPER: What's this? Oh, will you look at that? Marmite crumpets, my favourite. I knew you lot were up to something. Bless you all, how lovely… (*The song finishes.*)

JANIE: Blow them out then.

ROPER: What, all of them?

LINDEN: There's only eight.

JOSEFA: And don't forget to make a wish.

ROPER: A wish? But I got everything I want right here.

JANIE: Then just blow them out then.

ROPER: Righty-o.

> *ROPER blows out the candles. JANIE applauds and sits on the ground, hugging ROPER's leg. LINDEN sits. JOSEFA puts two crumpets on each of the smaller plates and distributes them…*

LINDEN: Happy Birthday, Grandad.

ROPER: Thank you, Linden.

JANIE: We would have done seventy candles but we thought you might die blowing them out.

ROPER: Very thoughtful. (*JOSEFA gives ROPER his crumpets.*) Ooh, thank you. Now, here's the best bit. Sucking the

Marmite off the bottom of the candles. (*He does this.*) Delicious.

JOSEFA starts clearing up.

JANIE: Speech.

ROPER: What's that, you want a speech?

JANIE: Speech.

LINDEN: But nothing weird.

ROPER: A speech, well, as it happens, I did prepare a few words…

JANIE: Here we go.

ROPER: Let's see if I can remember them, shall we? In my old age. (*He clears his throat.*) These last seventy years I've had a great many astonishing experiences. I've wrestled with man-eating leopards in the Himalayan foothills.

LINDEN: No you haven't.

ROPER: I've feasted with sultans and drunk the juice of many an exotic fruit. I've sung for the Queen, broke two world records and learnt and forgotten many foreign languages. I've even been in love.

JANIE: Stop clearing up, Josefa. Come and listen.

JOSEFA stops clearing up. She stands behind LINDEN, stroking his head…

ROPER: But these last two months have topped the lot thanks to the calibre of you three individuals.

LINDEN: Where's your bracelet?

JOSEFA: I took it off.

ROPER: And though we are a team, I'd like, with permission, to pay tribute to each of you separately.

JANIE: I love you, Roper. And I'm going to kiss your knee. (*She kisses his knee.*)

ROPER: Josefa. You've shown great generosity to us all and it's no secret you do the lion's share of the work about the place. Alongside Blossom, you're the kindest and most graceful woman I ever met and for that I thank you. Please, raise a crumpet to Josefa.

ALL: (*They raise their crumpets.*) To Josefa. (*They take a bite.*)

ROPER: Linden. You're not only my grandson, you're also my closest friend. I'm so lucky... (*He fights back tears.*)

JANIE: Don't cry, you pussy.

ROPER: I'm so lucky to have seen you grow up, Linden, from the tiny, burping baby of yesteryear, to the fine young gentleman of today. And I use the word gentle-man advisedly, because that's what you are, and it's a fabulous thing to be.

JOSEFA: Roper, you're so lovely.

ROPER: To Linden.

ALL: (*They raise their crumpets.*) To Linden. (*They take a bite.*)

ALUN appears on the pavement. He is baffled by what he is seeing.

ROPER: And last but not least, Janie, who is what I call 'a pocket dynamo' /

ALUN: Josefa?

ROPER: Oh.

JOSEFA: Alun. Hi.

Pause.

ALUN: I'm interrupting. I'll come back.

JOSEFA: No... Have a seat...

ALUN: No, I'll come back.

JOSEFA: Honestly, sit down. It's Roper's birthday.

ALUN: Sorry?

JOSEFA: Roper. He's seventy.

ALUN: Oh. Congratulations.

ROPER: Please, take the weight off.

ALUN: Really?

JOSEFA: Honestly.

ALUN: Thank you. (*He sits.*)

JOSEFA: Everyone, this is Alun. He's a doctor. We met when I was /

JANIE: Yeah, I know, it's him what ripped my head open?

JOSEFA: Don't be rude.

ROPER: It's very nice to meet you, Alun. In fact, I've got a problem with my groin muscles. (*Pretending he is about to drop his shorts.*) Wouldn't mind taking a look, would you, Doc?

LINDEN: Grandad.

ROPER: He knows I'm joking.

JANIE: Who's being rude? It's him what butted in when Roper was doing his speech.

ROPER: That's all right, I can finish it later. (*JANIE is unimpressed.*) Or I can finish it now, I'm sure Alun wouldn't mind.

ALUN: No.

JANIE: (*Gets up. Not angry, just sad.*) Don't bother.

ROPER: Oh, come on, love, don't be upset.

JANIE: I knew we wouldn't get to my bit.

ROPER: Don't go, you ain't finished your crumpets.

JANIE: I ain't hungry. (*She leaves.*)

LINDEN: I'll go after her.

JOSEFA: Don't be gone too long. We're having lamb, remember.

LINDEN follows JANIE, leaving just the adults. Pause.

ALUN: Sorry. I've broken up your party.

ROPER: That's okay. It was all over bar the shouting. Well, I think I'll go and sort out my knick-knack box. Make space for my new screwdrivers.

JOSEFA: Don't feel like you have to go.

ROPER: No, I'll feel better when it's done. Let you two catch up and so forth.

JOSEFA: Okay.

ROPER goes into the house, taking his new screwdrivers. ALUN and JOSEFA are alone. ALUN is still confused by the situation he has walked into.

JOSEFA: This is a surprise.

ALUN: Yeah…

JOSEFA: How are you?

ALUN: I'm fine. You?

JOSEFA: Fine.

ALUN: I'm sorry I've not been in touch.

JOSEFA: That's okay. I wasn't…expecting /

ALUN: No, listen, I've been in Germany. For six weeks. I've been doing this research project.

JOSEFA: Oh…

ALUN: It was kind of a spur of the moment thing. Someone dropped out at the last minute. I only got back yesterday.

JOSEFA: Right. (*JOSEFA softens.*) So what were you researching?

ALUN: A few things. Mainly babies that have difficulty making new skin cells.

JOSEFA: That sounds interesting.

ALUN: Yeah, it was. But hard. A lot of the children we saw, they were in a lot of pain. Really terrible pain. Quite painful to witness.

JOSEFA: Right.

ALUN: Children with a lot of skin missing. From their bodies. And heads disproportionate to their bodies. Quite painful to see. (*Pause.*) I didn't realise you lived with Janie. And other people.

JOSEFA: I didn't. I mean, it happened when I came out of hospital.

Pause.

ALUN: Right.

Pause.

JOSEFA: So, you don't ever get used to it?

ALUN: Get used to what?

JOSEFA: Other people's pain. With the passing of time, you've not become dead to it?

Pause.

ALUN: No. I think, if anything, it accumulates. Like lead or something.

Pause.

JOSEFA: Would you like to come inside?

ALUN: Is that okay?

JOSEFA: Of course. Come through.

They go into the house. Scene ends.

2 : 2

The graveyard. There are a few dead leaves on the ground. JANIE and LINDEN are a bit bored. LINDEN is sitting against a gravestone. It reads:

REST IN PEACE
CHERYL JANE INCHMORE
1.10.1950 – 1.10.2004
AN ANGEL IN ALL BUT NAME SHE WAS
LOOK AFTER HER, JESUS

JANIE is sitting against an adjacent gravestone. It reads:

JULIAN JENKS
1971 – 2004
HE DIED CLIMBING

JANIE has a smart, turquoise handbag that jars with the scruffiness of the rest of her outfit. She keeps it with her for the remainder of the play.

JANIE: Anus.

LINDEN: Who is?

JANIE: Him. The brain ripper. Interrupting Roper when he was in full flow.

LINDEN: Not on purpose. You're just miffed it was your section got interrupted.

JANIE: So would you be. (*JANIE cheers up and mounts LINDEN.*) Anyway, I don't care. Happy as tits I am at the moment. It's like my blood's doing star jumps. I jumped in bed with Roper this morning, yeah? And I bit his ear and he just gurgled like some fat fucking baby, sweet as tits. It's like a family only better, ain't it?

They kiss. This is clearly a regular thing now. JANIE grinds. INGER arrives. She watches for a moment then kicks JANIE off LINDEN.

JANIE: Oi.

INGER: Howdy doo, Asian children, how are things?

JANIE: Fuck off, Inger.

INGER: Yeah, I won't shake your hand, Lind, I ain't overly partial of anchovy paste. Pardon me interrupting a sexual act.

JANIE: You didn't.

INGER: Yeah right, so why's Lind got a stiffy like a bog brush?

LINDEN draws his knees up to his chest.

Serious, Lind, what you doing? She ain't even hygienic. Had a shit in a locker at school, weren't it?

JANIE: So?

INGER: So you ain't hygienic's what I'm explaining to your lover. 'Cos what did you even do, shit in your hand and sploink it in with your hand? Or did you wriggle your bony little bumcheeks through the metal doorway's what I'm saying, 'cos either way ain't overly hygienic.

JANIE: Fuck off, Inger.

INGER: No you fuck off, Wolf Girl. Remember that, Lind? Sir holds up that picture of that girl grew up with wolves so I shout 'Janie' and everyone totally utterly messes themselves, even Sir.

JANIE: Er, that didn't happen?

INGER: Yes it did, and a mouse ran out your hair the same day.

JANIE: No it didn't.

INGER: It did, Janie.

JANIE: A mouse?

INGER: Yes, Janie, a mouse. Accept and move on. (*Pause.*) So is it true what people been saying? About you two and your Grandad, Lind, all shacked up with Miss Button?

LINDEN: Kind of.

JANIE: Don't tell her.

INGER: Fuck off, I'm interested. (*Pause.*) So, do you like…sit round a table or eat off trays?

JANIE: Eh?

LINDEN: Sometimes we sit down.

INGER: And what about after that? Do you play like board games?

LINDEN: Not really.

INGER: Who washes the clothes?

LINDEN: Miss does.

INGER: That is weird, man. The whole thing.

JANIE: Yeah, it's called loving other people?

INGER: Oh, so you all love each other, do you, Janie?

JANIE: Er, yes?

INGER: You all make love to each other, do you?

JANIE: Er, there's a sizeable difference between those two things?

INGER: I bet you do. Bet Miss makes you chew on her nips and all. 'Linden, will you chew on my nipples please? While I sip my cup of cappuccino please?' Like corks off wine bottles she's got. I saw them on Activities Week. After potholing. One's pink like a shrimp, other's black as Lind. Is she like the mummy pig and you're the little sucky piglets?

JANIE: God, you're crude.

INGER: So?

JANIE: So don't be 'cos you're wrong. The only relationship is Linden and I.

INGER: Yeah, does it not ever occur to you, Janie, how not even interested I am in your Asian little life? I'm here to talk to Lind.

INGER turns her attention to LINDEN and does her best to ignore JANIE.

Thing is, Lind, I need something.

JANIE: Yeah, medicine for the brain.

INGER: 'Cos my sister's got this naming ceremony, 'cos they reckon she might die? So I got to get her a gift.

JANIE: Inger, your sister's already got a name. It's Holly. We done a whole fun run called 'Run For Holly'.

INGER sticks a finger up in JANIE's direction as she speaks. JANIE returns the gesture.

INGER: Will you get me something, Lind? 'Cos they reckon she might die's the thing. So will you steal me something?

LINDEN: Sorry, Inger. I don't steal no more.

INGER: Oh go on, though. It's for a good cause. They reckon she might die. I'd do it myself but I got banned from the shopping centre, didn't I? Got CCTV on me. Second I go past the chip shop it's like whoooop-whoooop-whoooop. (*The fingers go down.*) And I can't give her chips, can I? I can't give her saveloy and chips so they go 'I name it Holly' then I smack a big bag of chips in her face, can I? (*INGER finds this hilarious.*)

JANIE: Then go to the shops you ain't been banned from.

INGER: And get her what, cookware? Please steal me something.

LINDEN: If you give me the money, I'll buy you something.

JANIE: No you won't.

INGER: I'm skint. Go on, stealing's what you're best at.

JANIE: You deaf or something? He doesn't want to do it.

INGER: (*Touches LINDEN.*) Please, though /

JANIE: (*Kicks INGER's hand away from LINDEN.*) Excuse me, anus, you deaf? He doesn't want to.

INGER turns on JANIE. JANIE knows she is in trouble, but it is too late to back down.

INGER: What you call me?

JANIE: You heard, I called you a anus.

INGER: Called me a what?

JANIE: I called you a anus.

INGER: What you call me?

JANIE: I called you a well-rough, psychotic, Danish anus.

INGER grabs JANIE by the throat.

INGER: (*Shaking JANIE.*) Do not you. Rudely refer. You peculiar-smelling bitch. To me. Again. Like that again. Ever. (*She releases JANIE.*) So, you steal something, Lind, of value, and you give it me, yeah? Or else, 'cos I'm telling you, I am not dicking about now.

JANIE: Else what?

INGER: Just else, all right?

JANIE: Else what?

INGER: Just else.

JANIE: (*Still in pain.*) You can't just say 'just else', be specific.

INGER: All right. Else I get one of Holly's hypodermics… You know what one of them is, don't you, Lind? And I fill it with Worcester Sauce. And I track down Linden's strangely white grandad. And I whack the needle through the centre of his kneecap. And I squeeze. That okay for you, Wolf Girl?

ROPER: (*Off.*) You two.

INGER: Ooh, look at that. Speak of the paedophile.

ROPER appears with a walking stick. INGER adopts a peculiar, prim persona.

ROPER: Come on, you two. Josefa's doing lamb, remember.

INGER: Oh, really? Does she inject Worcester Sauce in?

ROPER: Eh?

INGER: Does she inject Worcester Sauce in the leg of it?

ROPER: I don't know. I never heard of that. I'll ask her, shall I? (*Pause, ROPER baffled.*) Come on, you pair. Time waits for nobody.

ROPER heads off. INGER wiggles the tip of her tongue at JANIE. LINDEN and JANIE follow ROPER off. INGER bites one of her hands. Scene ends.

2:3

ALUN is in the dragon room. JOSEFA watches ALUN as he looks at all the amazing stuff, just as fascinated as ROPER and JANIE were.

ALUN: It's amazing. Where did it all come from? (*No answer.*) Josefa, where did /

JOSEFA: It came from my mum.

ALUN looks at JOSEFA. She seems fragile. Pause.

ALUN: Right.

JOSEFA: She was actually...quite an incredible woman. She did a lot of travelling in her twenties. On her own mostly. Before that was normal for a woman. She spent quite a long time in Japan and places. She collected most of it then. Because she loved that kind of thing. Eastern mythology and that kind of thing.

ALUN: Right.

JOSEFA: Then when she died, she left it all to me. I try to keep it nice in case she's looking down.

ALUN: It looks beautiful.

JOSEFA: Thank you. (*Pause.*) Are you okay?

ALUN: Me?

JOSEFA: You've been seeming kind of startled.

ALUN: I am startled.

JOSEFA: Since you got here.

ALUN: Have I?

Pause.

JOSEFA: Is it the way we live? It's not as strange as it looks /

ALUN: No, it's not that. Although I was surprised…when I got here. To see the way you are with each other. But it's not just that.

JOSEFA: So what is it, then?

Pause.

ALUN: Okay, I'm a Christian. I never told you that. I don't tell many people. I don't go to church but I'm a Christian.

JOSEFA: That's okay.

ALUN: No, I haven't finished. (*Pause.*) I think you have to think about the signals you're giving. To God.

JOSEFA: What do you mean?

Pause.

ALUN: The way I see it… You want a baby, don't you? And God's made that difficult. He saw someone of real courage and strength, and for His own reasons, which are not, as I see it, ours to question, He's testing that strength. By placing obstacles in your path. And he wants to see your response.

63

JOSEFA: Okay.

ALUN: Okay, I'm just not sure what He'd make of your response. I just wonder if, by mothering these people, who aren't your children… I wonder if He might not like that. It's a really kind thing to do, but I wonder if, by fostering these people, it might seem to God like you're dodging the issue. Or like you've found a new path, so you no longer need His intervention. (*Pause.*) Have I upset you?

JOSEFA: I just think your idea of God…it's very different to mine. Like why are His choices not ours to question? And why does He need to test my strength? He must know what I can withstand because He gave me my strength. And… I mean… Surely he doesn't watch over us all as closely as that?

ALUN: Why not?

JOSEFA: Well, it's like Father Christmas. How could he possibly keep tabs on every child?

ALUN: But Josefa, this is God. And God's not a person, is He? He's nothing like a person. He's everywhere. And He's beyond time. And He /

JOSEFA: Sorry, this…

ALUN: What?

JOSEFA: This… It feels strange. Why are you here?

ALUN: What do you mean?

JOSEFA: I don't know why you're here.

ALUN: You wrote your address. In the 'thank you' card you left for me.

JOSEFA: Just to turn up though. After two months. And straight away…talking about… What are you doing here?

Pause as ALUN searches hard for the right words and for the courage to say them.

ALUN: Okay, when we first met…you were in so many different kinds of pain. And that upset me. (*Pause.*) Then, when I got your card…what you wrote…it was like…in those five, six conversations we had… It was like I'd taken some of that pain away. Which gave me a feeling I'd never had before.

JOSEFA: You're a doctor, you spend your life taking pain away.

ALUN: But this wasn't physical. This was… (*He holds a palm against his heart, then holds it close to her heart.*) But I only got some of it. The pain. I didn't get all of it. So… I don't know. I think… I think I'm here to finish what I started. To try to take the rest of the pain away.

JOSEFA: But the pain's already gone. Can't you see that? The pain's already beginning to go. What we have here, it feels right. It feels /

JANIE comes into the room.

JANIE: Er, what's going on?

JOSEFA: Janie. What are you doing in here?

JANIE: 'What's he doing in here?' more like.

JOSEFA: Don't be rude.

ALUN: It's all right, I'm used to it.

JANIE: Yeah, I bet you are.

JOSEFA: Where are the others?

JANIE: Buying some peas to go with the lamb?

JOSEFA: I haven't put it on yet.

JANIE: Why not? It's two o'clock. (*Pause.*) What's going on?

JOSEFA: Nothing.

JANIE: Something's different, what's he done?

JOSEFA: Don't be silly.

JANIE: Look at me.

JOSEFA: I am looking at you.

JANIE looks into JOSEFA's eyes. She kisses JOSEFA's mouth and then bites her lip – a declaration of territory.

Janie.

JANIE sticks a finger up at ALUN as she leaves the room…

JANIE: You still here?

She is gone. JOSEFA and ALUN look at one another. JOSEFA looks away. Scene ends.

2:4

JOSEFA's front garden. Evidence of decadence is now everywhere – wine bottles, some holding half-burnt candles, a disposable barbecue, a knackered sun lounger. There is a square of soil where once there was a concrete slab. LINDEN is planting daffodil bulbs in the soil. ROPER is sitting on a chair. Pause.

ROPER: I got a letter through the other day, Linden. From your mum.

LINDEN: (*Stops digging.*) What's it say?

ROPER: I'll read it out, shall I?

Pause. ROPER takes out a letter and reads…

'Roper.' She never calls me Dad. 'Roper. Why do you say I live in a boat when I live in a cottage? I never lived in a boat except for one fortnight and that was a houseboat and even if I did what does it even matter if something floats or not. What I'm saying is things are settled now. Four whole months without a single slip so my thought is Linden should come live in Honeybourne with me.' (*Pause.*) 'Me and Don are giving it one more go and the pain is gone, so are the nightmares for both of us so my thought is Linden should come and live with me in Honeybourne so we can start our lives again then can't we? I'll be better at it now.

And there is a chicken factory he could work at or he could catch a bus to the college I phoned so talk to him but don't say I live on a boat because that was just one fortnight and we are completely off the drugs. Joyce.'

Pause.

LINDEN: When did it all start, Grandad? With the drugs?

ROPER: Ten years?

Pause.

LINDEN: Why don't we talk about it? I wish we could talk about it. Without… (*LINDEN jabs at his own throat, suggesting a kind of blockage.*)

ROPER: That's my fault, not yours. That's my failure. I find it hard to think about. Let alone talk about. Especially to you. (*ROPER stands.*) Now the work's all done, I reckon I'll start sleeping at the flat again. Give you space to think about what you want to do.

LINDEN: It's difficult, Grandad. 'Cos that's like my real family? But what we got here's good too. I just want like…a peaceful family unit.

ROPER: (*Rests a hand on LINDEN's head.*) Be like half my heart sliced out and buried in that soil if you went away, Linden.

ROPER goes into the house. Scene ends.

2:5

A short while later. LINDEN digs at the square of soil. INGER appears on the pavement.

INGER: Howdy doo, Lind. So, did you get me something for the ceremony?

LINDEN goes into the house. He comes out with a plastic bag and gives it to INGER. She pulls out an artificial holly wreath.

INGER: Fuck's that?

LINDEN: A wreath. I bought it for the ceremony.

INGER: Er, why?

LINDEN: For you to give. 'Cos Holly's her name and that's what it's made of.

INGER: Er, wreaths are for dead people? For nailing to coffins? It's like saying 'hurry up and die'.

LINDEN: Not always. What about Christmas?

INGER: Well, it ain't Christmas either, is it? (*She throws the wreath at him.*) Penis, what is wrong with you? I meant a bracelet or a spoon or a white fucking bible. And steal it, I said.

LINDEN: Why have I got to steal for? I already told you I ain't going back to stealing.

INGER: Yeah, stealing's your fucking talent, I already told you that.

LINDEN: Yeah, and I told you I don't steal no more. My grandad's going to have ten heart attacks if I get done again. It's Young Offenders next time. I ain't doing it, totally no way.

INGER: All right, Lind, calm down, fuck me. (*Pause.*) After all, there's stealing and stealing if you know what I mean?

LINDEN: Inger, I don't ever know what you mean.

INGER: Well, there's thieving from shops and there's thieving from persons and or persons, ain't there? Miss must have items of value.

LINDEN: Eh?

INGER: Go on.

LINDEN: Totally no way.

INGER: Totally yes way though, 'cos this is what you need. You're getting too snagged up in all this family cack. You got to steal to keep in touch with the reality of being, else you'll get like Wolf Girl, distant from reality.

LINDEN: No, I ain't stealing off her, totally no way. You might as well get fond of the wreath.

INGER: Pardon, Lind.

LINDEN: I said I ain't stealing off her, no way, I ain't doing it, so you might as well get fond of the wreath.

LINDEN holds out the wreath. INGER does not take it.

INGER: That's okay, Lind. You don't got to steal off Miss Button.

LINDEN: Good, 'cos it ain't going to happen.

INGER produces a large syringe filled with Worcester Sauce.

Got to say though, Lind, it's going to give him a lot of pain. Like sugary burnt vinegar it is, leave a well nasty splodge up his leg it will. Sting like fucking acid, he won't half scream. That what you want for your Grandad? (*Clutches her head.*) 'Cos that's what I'll do, I'll smash it through his kneecap, I fucking swear, you get headaches?

LINDEN: Eh?

INGER: I get these well sharp headaches. I get this thought about if the people don't need air, so the people's got no lungs, so nothing goes in and out, then my head starts stabbing like total madness, you ever get that?

LINDEN: No.

INGER: Kills like I got petrol in my head.

Pause. She opens her eyes and pockets the syringe. The pain begins to subside. JANIE comes out of the house.

JANIE: Er, what's she doing here?

INGER: Er, I was talking to Linden?

JANIE: Well don't.

INGER: Free country last time I looked.

JANIE: Yeah, free country, not a free patio, so fuck off.

INGER: No need to be impolite, Janie.

JANIE: (*Prim.*) Inger, will you please depart please?

INGER: Yeah, when I feel like it.

JANIE: No, fuck off now or I'll get Miss.

INGER: How old are you?

JANIE: Sixteen, fuck off now or I'll get Miss.

INGER: Why, what's she doing in there, touching herself?

JANIE: No, she's staring at a picture of you and puking.

INGER: God, you're crude.

JANIE: So are you, remove yourself, you reek.

INGER: I'm actually going?

JANIE: Go then.

INGER: Bye, Lind.

LINDEN: Bye, Inger.

JANIE: Don't say bye to her.

INGER: Bye, Wolf Girl.

JANIE: Yeah, farewell, anus.

INGER: Farewell, bitch.

JANIE: Farewell, fucked-up Danish moose.

> *INGER wiggles the tip of her tongue at JANIE and goes.*
>
> (*Calls.*) Bitch.

INGER: (*Off.*) Piss-flaps.

JANIE: (*Calls.*) Bitch. (*Pause.*) I ain't keen on that girl.

Pause. JANIE launches herself at LINDEN, hugging and kissing him.

LINDEN: Don't.

JANIE: Why not? Kiss me.

LINDEN: (*Pushing her away.*) No.

Pause. LINDEN is distressed.

JANIE: What's the matter, baby?

LINDEN: I don't want to any more.

JANIE: Eh?

LINDEN: Me and you. I don't want to.

JANIE: Don't be a twonk. (*Pause.*) Eh? (*Pause.*) But you adore me.

LINDEN: So?

JANIE: So what sprung this on?

LINDEN: Nothing did.

JANIE: What sprung this on? We only did it two hours ago, what sprung this on? I'd murder a old lady with my hands for you.

LINDEN: I don't want you to.

JANIE: Then tell me what sprung this on. (*Pause.*) Is this Inger?

LINDEN: No.

JANIE: She been making threats? She's just a jealous psycho, she ain't going to do no harm, please don't be obedient to her.

LINDEN: I ain't.

JANIE: You're getting rid of me.

LINDEN: Not 'cos of Inger.

JANIE: Then what 'cos of? (*Pause.*) What 'cos of?

LINDEN: It's like… For a family unit…

JANIE: Eh?

LINDEN: Peaceful family unit…

JANIE: What you on about?

LINDEN: It's like we're this peaceful family unit, only we ain't a real family 'cos two of us, the boy and girl, keep having sex the whole time.

JANIE: We're the young ones, it's natural we're the ones in love.

LINDEN: Not for a family unit. People in families don't do that.

JANIE: Er, what about mums and dads?

LINDEN: Yeah, but we're the brother and sister, so it ain't natural. Specially not like we do it. I got bruises and bite-marks all over me.

JANIE: You said you like all that.

LINDEN: Yeah, but we're the brother and sister. And spending forty minutes a day with your dick in your sister's mouth… and her finger waggling round up your anus…like we just did…it ain't natural.

JANIE: Wasn't forty minutes.

LINDEN: Was almost, I could see my clock radio. And Josefa's drifting away already, ain't she?

JANIE: No.

LINDEN: She is, she hardly looks at me suddenly. She wants a proper family unit. Just be my twin sister instead, yeah?

LINDEN goes inside. Scene ends. JANIE looks up. Autumn leaves fall from the sky.

2:6

JANIE is picking up dead leaves and putting them in a plastic carrier bag. The bag is quite well stuffed. JOSEFA appears in the doorway with a cup of tea. Not seeing JANIE at first, she sits on the step.

JOSEFA: What are you doing?

JANIE: It's for you. I'm collecting the leaves. For the first years' first lesson.

JOSEFA: I don't do that lesson any more. I get them to draw each other instead.

JANIE: Fine. (*JANIE drops the bag.*) I was only trying to be of a help.

JANIE lies against JOSEFA, resting her head in her lap. JOSEFA is uncomfortable. JANIE sucks one of JOSEFA's fingers.

JOSEFA: Don't do that, it's not hygienic.

JOSEFA takes her finger from JANIE's mouth. Pause. JANIE tries again.

Stop it.

JANIE: I like it.

JOSEFA: You're not a baby.

JANIE: I'm your baby.

JOSEFA: Don't be silly.

JANIE: (*Trying to suck.*) I'm your baby and you're my mummy.

JOSEFA pulls her finger away.

Ow, no need to fracture my fucking gums. I have got gum disease, you know.

JOSEFA stands and begins emptying the dead leaves onto the ground in big handfuls…

What are you doing? (*No answer.*) Don't you get it? It's a natural family unit again. Me and Linden, we ain't boy and girlfriend, we're twins. Natural family unit with you as the mum, like how you want it.

JOSEFA: It's not about you and Linden.

JANIE: Yes it is, else why did we split up? (*Pause.*) Else why did we split up?

The bag is now empty. Pause.

JOSEFA: I'm scared. I'm scared that if I live like this... I'll be misunderstood.

JANIE: By who?

JOSEFA: By the future?

Pause as JOSEFA begins to redistribute the leaves by kicking them.

JANIE: Is this Alun? Is it him filling your head with all this? Is he why you're drifting away? (*No answer.*) Josefa, don't listen. Please, it don't work without you. Roper's hardly here now neither 'cos of fuck knows why. Please, just promise that things can stay like before.

JOSEFA: Nothing stays the same forever.

JANIE: Then promise you won't shut us out for no reason.

JOSEFA stops what she is doing and looks at JANIE.

JOSEFA: I won't.

JANIE: What, won't shut us out or won't promise?

JOSEFA: I won't shut you out for no reason. I promise.

JANIE: Swear on your mother's grave.

JOSEFA: On my mother's grave, I swear.

Josefa walks away. Janie calls after her...

JANIE: I don't believe you. He's stealing you from us, I can feel it.

Scene ends. JANIE looks up into the sky. Autumn leaves fall from the sky. Pause. The paddling pool falls from the sky. It is just a couple of puffs from being fully inflated.

2:7

JANIE is blowing up the pool. LINDEN and ROPER stand over her. Four chairs surround the pool. JANIE is drunk.

LINDEN: It's starting to rain.

JANIE: No it ain't.

LINDEN: I can feel it on my hand.

JANIE: Don't be a child, Linden.

ROPER: Is a bit cold, love. For feet in the water /

JANIE: Yeah, I'm going to use warm water so shut your fucking gobs. There's people on this planet live in houses made of snow. Think of them. Sit down.

The boys sit on the chairs. LINDEN looks up at the ominous sky. JOSEFA arrives on the step. JANIE closes the valve and produces a quarter-drunk bottle of Hayden's Excellent Gin.

JANIE: You'll be delighted to hear I've enquired a bottle of gin. Who'd like to have some? Josefa?

JOSEFA: No, thank you.

JANIE: Roper? How's about a drink being as you ain't hardly ever here no more?

ROPER: Not for me, thank you.

JANIE: Linden, stop looking at the sky.

LINDEN: (*Looking at the sky.*) I ain't looking at the sky.

JANIE: You are, you're still doing it.

LINDEN: Yeah, 'cos it's nearly winter.

JANIE: So? Don't mean we can't have fun. Have a drink.

LINDEN: I don't want to.

JANIE: Fine then. More for me. (*She drinks.*)

ROPER: Steady /

> *ROPER pulls the bottle from JANIE's mouth.*

JANIE: Roper, tell a story.

ROPER: A story?

JANIE: Yeah, go on. Might as well, now I've dragged you here.

ROPER: I ain't really got any new ones.

JANIE: The ear one, do that.

ROPER: I can't, I ain't done the preparations.

JANIE: Then do a different one, Jesus fuck, just tell a story, I ain't asking you to knife a dog. (*No story is forthcoming.*) Fine, I'll tell one. It's about people trying to spoil a thing like you're all doing now.

LINDEN: I'm just cold.

JANIE: Yeah, and I'm just trying to make people happy so there's no need to hate me.

ROPER: We don't hate you, love.

JOSEFA: Actually, I need you all to go.

LINDEN: Eh?

JOSEFA: For the afternoon. Sorry. Alun's coming round, so /

JANIE: Who's Alun?

JOSEFA: Don't be silly.

JANIE: Oh, you mean Jesus Christ Super-Fucking-Anus.

JOSEFA: Yeah, well, anyway, he'll be here in a minute /

JANIE: No, I don't like him.

ROPER: Janie /

THE CRACKS IN MY SKIN: TWO

JANIE: No, he ain't coming round, I ain't keen on him.

ROPER: Love, it's not your house.

JANIE: Yes it is, and he ain't coming round. We're having a nice time here, I just blown up a paddling pool from scratch.

Pause. JANIE takes a gulp of gin. She lets out a spluttering cry as it burns her insides.

ROPER: Janie, love /

JANIE: No. It was all perfect till he turned up splattering on at her. Now she don't even look at us or speak. She don't even let me in the dragon room. She don't even stroke Linden's head no more and he loves her like a dog. Way more than he loves me. He don't love me at all, but he loves her like a dog and she don't even look at him. 'Cos of this man. It's cruel. He's stealing her and we're letting him. He ain't coming, he can kiss my tits.

ROPER: Now, come on /

JANIE: No /

ROPER: Be fair /

JANIE: I am being fair. (*Pause.*) All right, fine, he can come, just don't expect me to be here.

JANIE sticks a finger up and drinks the gin like it is water...

ROPER: Whoa, steady on /

ROPER pulls the bottle from JANIE. She screams, gin running down her, and runs off.

I'll go after her.

ROPER picks up his stick and follows JANIE. Pause.

LINDEN: Why don't you stroke my head no more?

JOSEFA: Because you're not a baby and I'm not your mum.

Pause.

LINDEN: Bitch.

LINDEN goes into the house. JOSEFA buries her head in her hands. ALUN appears.

ALUN: Josefa?

She starts to cry.

Hey, come on, what's the matter?

JOSEFA: It's all wrong.

ALUN: What is?

JOSEFA: What have I done?

ALUN: (*Strokes her hair.*) It's okay.

JOSEFA: I've been so stupid.

ALUN: No you haven't.

JOSEFA: I can't do this.

ALUN: Do what?

JOSEFA: Push them away. When my mum left me…

ALUN: Josefa, your mum died.

JOSEFA: I can't do it. To Linden. I can't. I've made such a big mistake.

He wipes away a tear. She takes his hand and kisses it. Pause. He takes their hands away from her face but continues to hold her hand.

ALUN: Come on, let's go somewhere. Let's go for a walk and talk about all this.

JOSEFA: Okay. (*He helps her up.*)

ALUN: Get a drink or something. Come on.

They walk away. Scene ends.

2:8

The graveyard. LINDEN sits against a gravestone. INGER approaches.
LINDEN does not look at her.

INGER: All right, Lind.

LINDEN: Inger.

INGER: Howdy doo, all right? (*Pause.*) I was just thinking about that occurrence, remember? When that cat got mangled in that razorwire fence, and we was all cheering 'cept you, 'cos you were like, 'Shit, I'm going to unmangle it, don't even care if it looks like I'm gay.'

LINDEN: So?

INGER: 'Cos I was like 'Lind, that is way gay,' but actually, fuck off, what you did was decent. I condone with your actions looking back. Lind, are you trying to be rude?

LINDEN: No.

INGER: Then look at me, Lind, 'cos I'm trying to be nice, so do not you be fucking rude to me, else I swear, I'll slice you with a razor cross your black fucking back, you got that? Man, what is it with you? I'm serious. (*Pause.*) So, did you get me something?

LINDEN takes JOSEFA's bracelet from his pocket. He gives it to INGER.

What's that?

LINDEN: It's a bracelet?

INGER: Yeah, but what's that on it?

LINDEN: It's a wyvern. It's like a dragon with a snakey tail.

INGER: It's good. Will she notice it gone?

No answer. INGER pockets the ornament.

Actually, Lind, the naming ceremony ain't happening.

LINDEN: No?

INGER: No, it got cancelled. So, the something to give, that weren't the actual purpose for saying let's meet up today.

LINDEN: What is then?

INGER: Well shut your trap and I'll tell you, won't I? (*Pause.*) Just I heard you saw finally sense. With regard to that strange creation you was plugging, is it true?

LINDEN: So what if it is?

INGER: Nothing, just well done. She is like some peculiar species, ain't she, that girl?

LINDEN: No.

INGER: Some way odd creature, stinks of compost, what was in your mind, man?

LINDEN: Nothing was.

INGER: That's what I'm saying. She's like some gone wrong form of life /

LINDEN: Shut up.

INGER: Tell me to shut up, I'll set your fucking clothes on fire, cut your fucking wrists up, fuck, my head, it kills.

INGER holds onto her head in pain.

LINDEN: You all right, Inger?

INGER: Yes, thank you. (*The pain subsides.*) But anyhows, you got a friend in me is the thing that I'm saying. If splitting up with Wolf Girl has maked you depressed.

LINDEN: Cheers, Inger.

INGER: 'Cos there is a reason, Lind. For why I selected you for the stealing.

LINDEN: Eh?

INGER: 'Cos that time last year? When me and you made love?

LINDEN: What about it?

INGER: Only my second ever time that was. So, yeah, actually… 'Cos to me it was special, yeah? I ponder on it all the time. On how you like… laid me down on the grass and leaves? (*Pause.*) On how you like kissed me round my shoulders? I think about it all the time. With the sun leaking down all gentle through the branches.

LINDEN: That was when we were like fourteen.

INGER: Yeah, but what I'm saying, Lind, if you want to do it again, only as my actual boyfriend this time /

LINDEN: Eh?

INGER: 'Cos you can. Even right now if you like. But as my actual boyfriend, yeah?

LINDEN: Inger, what you on about?

INGER: 'Cos I love you, don't I?

LINDEN: Eh?

INGER: I love you, don't I? That's why I selected you for the stealing, to get us close again.

LINDEN: You joking?

INGER: No. What? Just be my boyfriend, yeah?

LINDEN: I can't.

INGER: You can. You love me.

LINDEN: I don't.

INGER: You do. I'm fiery.

LINDEN: Inger, you threatened to hurt my grandad.

INGER: Yeah, as a joke?

LINDEN: You keep on threatening to hurt me.

INGER: Yeah, and I will if you don't stop acting like a penis. (*Pause.*) Please though, Lind. It's special to me, the way you touch. Please. (*LINDEN laughs.*) What?

LINDEN laughs some more. INGER laughs too.

What?

LINDEN: Just makes me laugh. It's like every girl suddenly just wants to have sex with me, like I'm totally suddenly irresistible.

INGER: 'Cos you are.

LINDEN: And every girl I've ever had sex with just wants to have non-stop sex with me for the rest of their whole life.

INGER: Yeah, it's called being sexy?

LINDEN: It's mental.

INGER: It's called being special. It's 'cos you're sensitive. And nice. Not to mention you got a penis nearly the size of a big shoe. (*Pause.*) So is it a yes then? 'Cos if I had a person in my life /

LINDEN: I don't want to /

INGER: 'Cos I'm tired of being the violent one, and if I had like a person in my life /

LINDEN: Inger /

INGER: 'Cos it ain't me, all the threats, it's a act. And 'cos of these headaches, else I'd be more gentle.

She tries to kiss and touch him.

Come on, Lind. Have sex with me. Please /

LINDEN: No. I ain't up for it /

INGER: You are.

LINDEN: Inger, I ain't even tempted. I totally wish we never even done it in the first place. Makes me feel sick to think of.

Pause. LINDEN sees that INGER is hurt.

Sorry, Inger, it's just a bit deranged. With all the threats and then… It ain't like you ain't nice looking. I just… Fuck, everything's going mental, man, everything's falling apart /

INGER: Man, you're one deadly fucking fond-of-yourself bitch, you are, Linden. Fuck is it with you? Reckon 'cos you're black-skinned it's your right to be loved or what?

LINDEN: No /

INGER: 'Cos I don't love you, I said it for effect, and if I had a brush made of metal I'd scrub the skin right off you till it's just a load of shreds. 'Everyone totally loves me, man. Everyone wants total non-stop sex with me, man.' No, they don't, not even your parents love you. It's genetic they should love you, still they don't.

LINDEN gets up to go. INGER pushes him and he trips and falls to the ground.

And just where do you think you're going? You ain't going nowhere, Lind. (*She kicks him.*) I hope your fucking head falls off, man. Bang nails up your nose-holes till you fucking well weep, you piece of turd on a pavement, I hate you. Only said be my boyfriend, no need to treat me like a piece of fucking insect.

INGER covers her eyes.

LINDEN: Don't cry, Inger.

INGER: I ain't crying.

LINDEN: Don't cry.

INGER: Why's no one choosing me?

LINDEN: Don't cry.

INGER: I ain't crying it's my headaches.

Pause.

LINDEN: All right, I'm going now.

INGER: (*Uncovers her eyes.*) No you ain't. Not without a gift.

LINDEN: Eh?

INGER: (*Sits on him.*) Not without a gift from me you ain't. (*Takes out the syringe.*) Not without a fucking gift.

LINDEN: Oh fuck.

INGER: (*Punching the needle repeatedly into LINDEN's leg, each stab bringing a scream from LINDEN.*) Not without a gift from me. Not without a gift. Not without a gift from me.

Scene 2:9 begins, overlapping.

Not without a fucking gift you ain't going. Not without a gift from Inger.

INGER runs away. LINDEN is in agony.

LINDEN: Oh fuck. Oh God, oh Jesus. Jesus fucking… Help me.

There is no-one around. LINDEN stands and runs away in great pain. Scene ends. The front door of the house slams shut.

2:9

The dragon room has been been wrecked. JOSEFA comes in. She looks around in shock at the chaos of broken ornaments and torn material. ALUN follows JOSEFA into the room. He is horrified…

ALUN: Who did this?

JOSEFA: Linden.

ALUN holds JOSEFA.

I don't want to see them any more.

Scene 2:10 begins, overlapping. JOSEFA kisses ALUN. He kisses back with passion then pulls back. ALUN and JOSEFA look at one another. They hear LINDEN bang on the door and shout out…

ALUN: I'll speak to him.

ALUN leaves the dragon room. JOSEFA feels her wrist. She is not wearing her bracelet. She realises that the bracelet has been taken. She slowly curls into a foetal position on the floor and listens to what is happening outside…

2:10

LINDEN arrives at the house. He is in extreme pain. He is dribbling and wailing and blood is soaking through his trousers. His words are not always clear. He bangs on the door.

LINDEN: Josefa. Josefa, please.

LINDEN backs away from the door and sits in the centre of the heart-shaped area of pebble. He throws pebbles at the door.

Josefa.

JANIE arrives.

JANIE: Eh?

LINDEN: Josefa.

JANIE: Eh, what's happened? What you done?

LINDEN: Inger done my leg.

JANIE: She done what?

LINDEN: With the needle, with the Worcester Sauce.

JANIE: Eh, you telling me that's blood? (*She grabs his leg and squeezes it.*) I'll murder that girl, I'll flaming well kill her.

LINDEN: (*Screams.*) What you doing?

JANIE: Sorry /

LINDEN: (*Screams.*) What you doing?

JANIE: Sorry, sorry, sorry. I'll get Josefa, shall I?

LINDEN: She ain't coming out.

JANIE: Josefa, come out, we need you.

LINDEN: She ain't coming.

JANIE: Eh? But you been stabbed.

LINDEN: The end of the needle's broke off in my leg.

JANIE: (*Thumps the door.*) Josefa, get outside, now /

LINDEN: Fuck.

JANIE: We need you, Linden's been stabbed, get outside /

LINDEN: I feel sick /

JANIE: Josefa /

LINDEN: I think I'm going to puke /

JANIE: It's all right, I'm here, just do big breaths, yeah?

LINDEN: Yeah…

JANIE: Nothing to worry about, yeah?

> *JANIE touches the wound again. LINDEN screams.*

> Sorry, sorry /

> *ALUN comes out of the house, closing the door behind him.*

> You, get Josefa, now.

ALUN: I'm really sorry, she doesn't want to see you.

JANIE: No, get Josefa, Linden's got stabbed.

ALUN: He's what?

JANIE: With a needleful of Worcester Sauce /

ALUN: (*Sees LINDEN's bloody leg.*) Right, okay /

JANIE: So get her.

ALUN: Linden, take your trousers off.

JANIE: You deaf, you poof? Get her.

ALUN: I'm a doctor.

JANIE: Get. Her.

ALUN: Come on, unbutton your trousers.

ALUN gives JANIE his phone and unbuttons LINDEN's trousers.

Janie, phone an ambulance.

JANIE: You not hearing me?

ALUN: Look, she doesn't want to see you, I'm really sorry /

LINDEN: Why not?

ALUN: You'll have to speak to her about that.

JANIE: Er, how can we?

LINDEN: Please /

ALUN: There's nothing I can do, she doesn't want to see you.

JANIE: Yeah, and why not?

ALUN has partially removed LINDEN's trousers. JANIE throws ALUN's phone to the ground and starts kicking at him.

JANIE: 'Cos of you, fucking bible-basher. All 'cos of you, bloody anus God-fucker.

ALUN: Okay, fine, I'll call the ambulance, and then I'll speak to her.

JANIE: Good, 'cos it's all your fault, so why don't you just do as you're told?

ALUN: I just said, I'll speak to her. I don't think she'll come but I'll try.

JANIE: Go on then. Go.

Fearing that JANIE will follow him through the door, ALUN goes down the passageway. LINDEN stands and starts to limp away. He is crying, still in real pain. JANIE stands in his way, holds him back, clings to him…

JANIE: Linden, what you doing?

LINDEN: Going.

JANIE: Eh? Linden, he's gone to get her.

LINDEN: So?

JANIE: So, she's going to come out.

LINDEN: No she ain't, 'cos I smashed up the dragon room.

JANIE: Eh?

LINDEN: And I stole her bracelet.

JANIE: What for?

LINDEN: To remind her how it feels.

JANIE: Linden…

LINDEN: To think something's yours then it's taken away.

JANIE: (*Stunned.*) Linden, you twonk.

LINDEN: I don't care, I'm going, get out of my way.

JANIE: But you done your leg, you got to rest, where you going?

LINDEN: Honeybourne.

JANIE: Eh? But you done your leg, you can't go there.

LINDEN: Why not?

JANIE: 'Cos I love you, we love each other /

LINDEN: Just get off, I do what I want, yeah?

JANIE: But Linden /

LINDEN: I said I do what I want.

LINDEN pushes JANIE away and runs off, holding his leg. There is blood on JANIE's fingers. She sucks hard on them. Pause. JANIE pounds the door and calls out…

JANIE: Josefa, Linden's gone. 'Cos of you, so open the door. Open it, you bitch, Linden's gone.

JOSEFA leaves the dragon room. Scene 2:9 ends. JANIE takes a packet of crisps from her bag. She opens it, empties the crisps onto the ground, defecates in the empty packet and posts it through the letterbox. She

THE CRACKS IN MY SKIN: TWO

takes the envelope from 1:7 and a pen from her bag. She writes on the envelope, pushes it through the letterbox and leaves. Scene ends.

2:11

Dusk. A tent on the top of a hill. JANIE's possessions are scattered untidily around the tent – her bag, a few items of clothing and shoes, some loose cassette tapes and CDs, some magazines and a heavy, clumsily sculpted, clay pineapple. It is dusk. JANIE is sitting amongst her possessions with her face buried in LINDEN's t-shirt from 1:6. ALUN arrives.

ALUN: Hello, Janie.

JANIE: (*She looks up at ALUN with hatred and astonishment.*) Go away.

ALUN: Can I sit with you?

JANIE: No, I just said, go away. (*He sits.*) Anus, I said go away.

ALUN: I don't want a fight.

JANIE: Then go. (*Pause.*) What do you want?

ALUN: To understand? (*Pause.*) Why?

JANIE: Why what?

ALUN: Why would you do that?

JANIE: Do what?

ALUN: Well, for a start, push your own faeces through her letterbox.

JANIE: How do you know it's mine, you been sniffing it?

ALUN: I don't understand why you'd do that. Josefa's a /

JANIE: Bitch.

ALUN: No /

JANIE: Yeah, she's a bitch, go away /

ALUN: No, she's a very kind person. She let you stay in her home. She took nothing in return /

JANIE: She's took everything, she's ate my whole life.

ALUN: She even gave you pocket money /

JANIE: Yeah, and now she's throwed us out for no reason. Like we're bits of fucking toenail.

ALUN: Not for no reason.

JANIE: What, 'cos Linden's thieved her bracelet and smashed her dragons? Fuck that, she's spat us out 'cos you've totally washed her brain is why. 'Cos you want to make love to her.

ALUN: That's not what I want.

JANIE: Yeah, right, course you don't. Well it's what she wants from you. She sees you as the dad.

Pause.

ALUN: I just wanted to help her be happy.

JANIE: Yeah, we'd already done that before you arrived. Me, Linden and Roper. You've just gone and brought the misery back. Do you really reckon you've been a success?

ALUN: I don't know…

JANIE: Do you really reckon you've been of a help? You reckon she's happy now?

ALUN: I don't know, maybe not, but listen /

JANIE: Her life's just gone from perfect to bad in sixty seconds, and it's totally, totally your fault.

ALUN: Okay, this isn't what I came here to talk about.

JANIE: Oh, I'm sorry, what did you come here to talk about? The price of anuses?

ALUN produces the envelope.

ALUN: (*Reads.*) 'Jesus is a fucking Paki.'

JANIE: So? 'Jesus is a fucking Paki.'

ALUN: I'm not telling you off, I'm just trying to understand.

JANIE: 'Jesus is a fucking Paki.' What don't you understand?

ALUN: Why you would write that.

JANIE: Why not?

ALUN: Well, for a start…it's racist.

JANIE: No it ain't.

ALUN: It is racist.

JANIE: I thought you thought Jesus was good.

ALUN: I do.

JANIE: So why is it racist? Just means Pakis are good.

ALUN: Because it's a racist word.

JANIE: What is?

ALUN: Paki.

JANIE: Then stop saying it then.

ALUN: Linden's black.

JANIE: Yeah, I actually noticed that when I made love to his body?

ALUN: Okay, fine. It's not just racist, it's also blasphemous.

JANIE: What's that mean?

ALUN: It's offensive to God. And to people that believe in God.

JANIE: Er, yeah, that was the kind of idea? 'Cos like… I despise you and you despise me? And God despises me and I despise God? And that's why I wrote it? And that's what I meant by the shit in the crisp packet? 'Cos shit's what you're made of? And it's also what God's made of?

ALUN: God doesn't hate you.

JANIE: Yeah he does, else why am I living in a tent? Why do the doors open up on me then slam?

ALUN: I don't know, but I know he loves you. You are an amazing person, Janie. You've got more spirit, more personality /

JANIE: Yeah, please don't try and make amends. Making things better ain't something you're good at.

JANIE tidies her possessions. ALUN watches her.

ALUN: We're a lot more similar than you realise.

JANIE: No we ain't.

ALUN: I know you're angry with me, but I promise you, me and you, we're a lot more similar than you realise. I was bullied at school, just like you.

JANIE: I ain't surprised.

ALUN: My parents didn't care about me, just like yours don't. And I've spent much of my life hurt that no one could see the good in me. Just like you have. But then I realised something.

JANIE: There is no good in you.

ALUN: All that love I felt and wanted to share /

JANIE: That's why they couldn't see it.

ALUN: Everything inside that I wanted others to see /

JANIE: Because there isn't any.

ALUN: God could see it all. (*JANIE laughs.*) I'm serious. We spend our lives hoping that someone someday might just catch a glimpse of what we have to offer, and all the while, He knows us better than we know ourselves /

JANIE: Please, just say sorry and fuck off, that's all I want.

ALUN: And all we have to do is believe in Him and we'll never feel lonely again.

JANIE: Yeah, right, fine, good.

ALUN: It doesn't even have to be Jesus. Worship whatever you like /

JANIE: Fine, I'll worship a mouldy flannel, will you go now please?

ALUN: But if you let God in, and I mean really let Him in, you will never feel lonely again. I promise, you will never feel lonely again. Never. (*Pause. JANIE is affected by these words.*) And Linden leaving, and Josefa… None of that will hurt so much. Because you'll know it's what He wants for them.

Pause.

JANIE: So, what about me then? 'Cos I ain't got a family. Just a dad what don't exist and a mum what calls me 'rat', they don't want me. I ain't even got a boyfriend now, I'm alone. Alone except a tent. What's God want for me?

Pause.

ALUN: I think He wants the same for you as He wants for me. That we should be alone.

JANIE: (*Fills with rage.*) But I don't want to be on my own. I don't want to be on my own. God can kiss my fucking tits, I don't want to be on my own.

ALUN: (*Reaches out to her.*) It's all right.

JANIE: Don't you touch me fucking dare fucking touch me. I hate you you cunt you fucking cunt I fucking hate you. I don't want to be on my own.

She grabs the clay pineapple and beats ALUN with it. It is a ferocious attack, the pineapple repeatedly coming down from above her head, smashing his face, shoulders and ribs…

I want love, I want love, I want love, I want love, I want love, I want love, I want love, I want love, I want love. I

93

want love. I don't want to be on my own. Never. I want love, real love.

JANIE stops, crying, exhausted. ALUN gets to his feet, clutching his bleeding face, literally holding it together with one hand. He holds his other arm awkwardly across his chest.

ALUN: It's all right. I understand.

ALUN goes. Scene ends.

2:12

Night time. The tent on the top of the hill. The mess outside the tent remains. ROPER approaches the tent. He is short of breath from climbing the hill. He knocks on the tent with his knuckle, making almost no sound.

ROPER: Love. (*Pause.*) It's me. It's Roper. (*Pause.*) Janie, love /

JANIE: What do you want?

ROPER: I've come for a visit, haven't I?

JANIE: I ain't coming out.

ROPER: Come on, little bear. Come on. I just walked up a hill for you, it ain't good for my hip.

JANIE: I don't care.

ROPER: Come on. (*Pause.*) Well, I ain't going nowhere till I've seen that daft little face of yours. I'll stand here till Christmas if I have to. Stand here till the end of time.

Pause. JANIE unzips the tent and sticks her head out.

There she is.

JANIE gets out of the tent and hugs ROPER.

Hey, what's all this? There you go. What's all this, eh?

He kisses her head. Pause.

JANIE: Linden's left us.

ROPER: It seems so.

JANIE: Bitch Inger done his leg.

ROPER: He's just lucky his parents are drug addicts. Infections from needles is their specialist subject. (*He lets go of her.*) Come on, let's have a tidy round, shall we?

ROPER tidies JANIE's things. She looks down at the town – a million orange lights.

Well, you gave that Alun a proper going over. Broke his ribs, smashed his face up. Snapped his thumb /

JANIE: I done him with my pineapple.

ROPER: Gashes, bruises, even swallowed a tooth, apparently.

JANIE: I ate a bit of him.

ROPER: Come here, your face needs a wash. (*He licks his finger and wipes blood from her face.*) Little blobs of blood.

They look down at the town.

It's a dangerous place to pitch a tent, top of a hill. Get yourself struck by lightning.

JANIE: Maybe I want to get struck by lightning. You ever wish you could fly, Roper?

ROPER holds JANIE's hand.

ROPER: I knew a chap who could fly, did I ever tell you this? Inky was his name. And all his life he'd had terrible eczema rashes, ever since from when he was a little baby.

JANIE: I get eczema.

ROPER: Then you'll know. Oof. Terrible, burning, itchy feeling. Up his back, down his neck, across his shoulders. In his ears. Crippling. But he was a great man was Inky, and he bore the pain with a big smile, and with great generosity of spirit until one day Inky woke to find his arms all covered in feathers. That's right, lovely, soft, white feathers, just like what a dove's got. All up his arms

95

they were, across his back and where his hair should have been. Everywhere, top to toe, and not itchy, just beautiful feathers. Feathers as white and soft as your beautiful young skin.

He kisses her hand.

So, what did Inky do? In the early morning sunlight, he walked to the top of a hill, this hill in fact. And he beated his beautiful wings. And he flew up and up and out and over the graveyard, over the houses and fields, followed a stream to a river, followed that river to the sea, then out across the ocean to a place called Sri Lanka where he lives to this day, in a lemon tree on the edge of a cricket pitch.

He kisses her hand again and holds it against his face.

JANIE: This is it now, Roper. Just me and you, bound together, tight as a knot. And nothing gets in, and nothing gets it spoilt, and nothing infects it, yeah?

ROPER: That's right.

JANIE: Tight as anything, like we got to breathe together, like we got the same lungs and blood cells and we only got one heart.

ROPER: One heart.

JANIE: Smash away the glass, first people ever. We'll smash it all away and love each other like people in stories. This is it now forever.

Scene ends. Play ends.